CHART HITS
OF 2021-2022

2 All Too Well
Taylor Swift

12 Cold Heart (PNAU Remix)
Elton John and Dua Lipa

21 Easy on Me
Adele

16 Fancy Like
Walker Hayes

33 Follow You
Imagine Dragons

28 Ghost
Justin Bieber

38 Happier Than Ever
Billie Eilish

46 Heat Waves
Glass Animals

58 If I Didn't Love You
Jason Aldean and Carrie Underwood

53 It'll Be Okay
Shawn Mendes

64 Love Again
Dua Lipa

70 My Universe
Coldplay x BTS

78 Permission to Dance
BTS

90 Shivers
Ed Sheeran

85 Stay
The Kid LAROI feat. Justin Bieber

96 We Don't Talk About Bruno
from ENCANTO

ISBN 978-1-70516-100-5

Visit Hal Leonard Online at
www.halleonard.com

Contact us:
Hal Leonard
7777 West Bluemound Road
Milwaukee, WI 53213
Email: info@halleonard.com

In Europe, contact:
Hal Leonard Europe Limited
42 Wigmore Street
Marylebone, London, W1U 2RN
Email: info@halleonardeurope.com

In Australia, contact:
Hal Leonard Australia Pty. Ltd.
4 Lentara Court
Cheltenham, Victoria, 3192 Australia
Email: info@halleonard.com.au

ALL TOO WELL

Words and Music by TAYLOR SWIFT
and LIZ ROSE

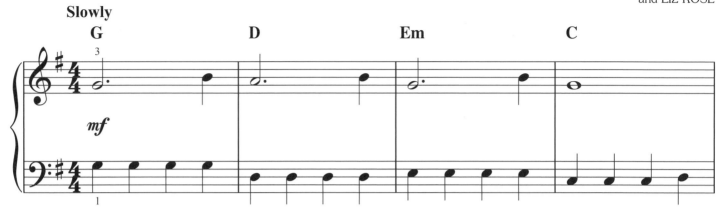

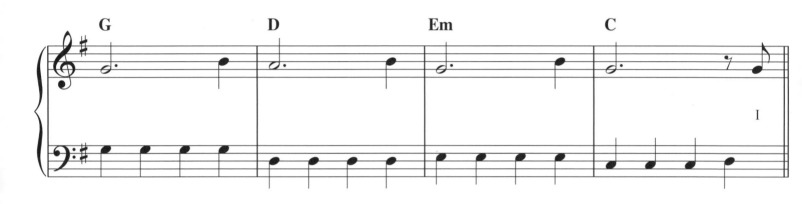

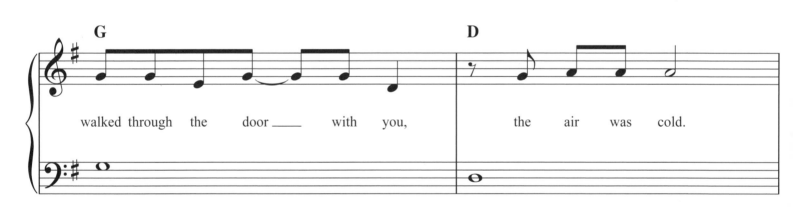

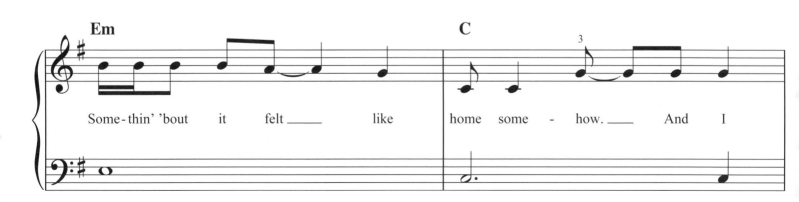

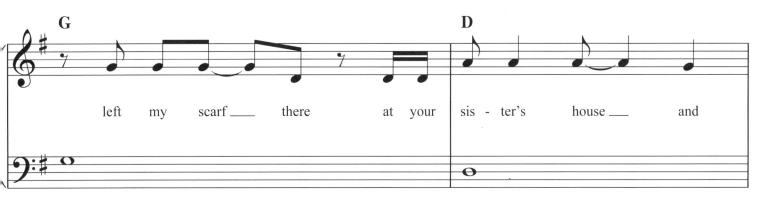

left my scarf ___ there at your sis - ter's house ___ and

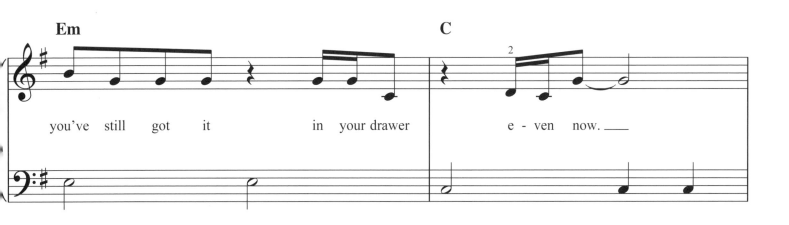

you've still got it in your drawer e - ven now. ___

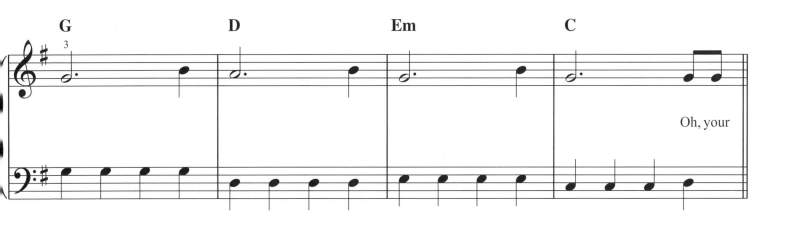

Oh, your

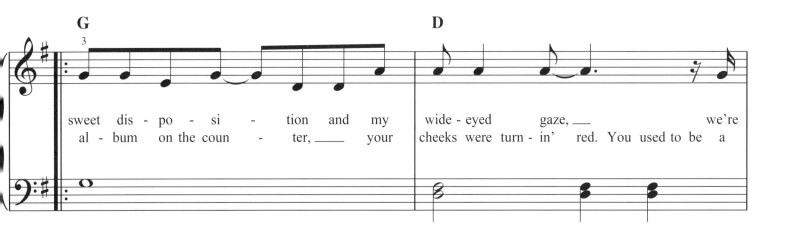

sweet dis - po - si - tion and my wide - eyed gaze, ___ we're
al - bum on the coun - ter, ___ your cheeks were turn - in' red. You used to be a

4

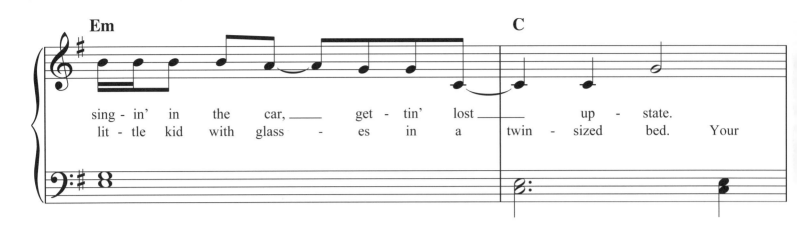

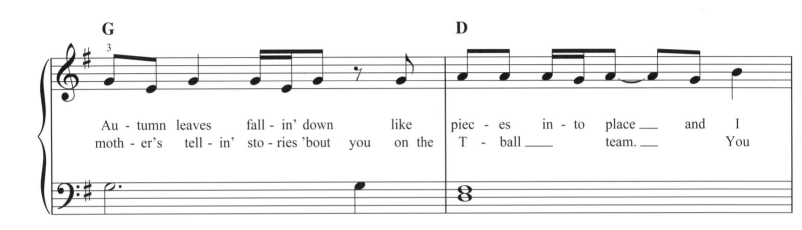

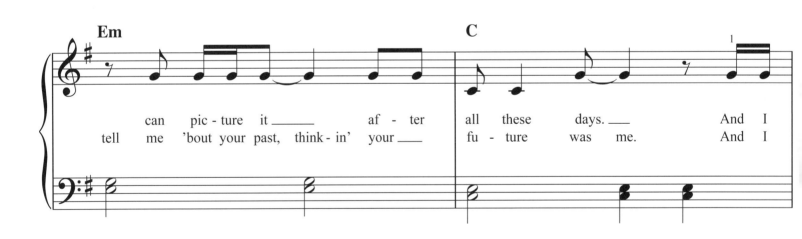

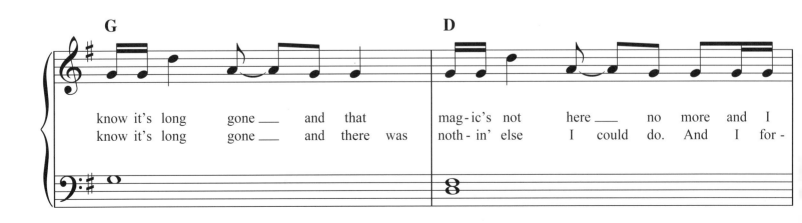

might be o - kay, ____ but I'm not
get a - bout you long e - nough to for - get

fine at all. _____
why I need - ed to. ____

'Cause there we are a - gain __ on that
'Cause there we are a - gain __ in the

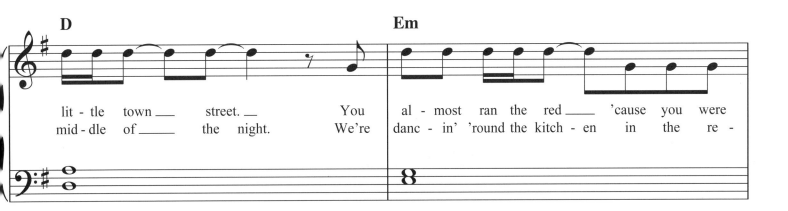

lit - tle town __ street. __ You
mid - dle of __ the night. We're

al - most ran the red __ 'cause you were
danc - in' 'round the kitch - en in the re -

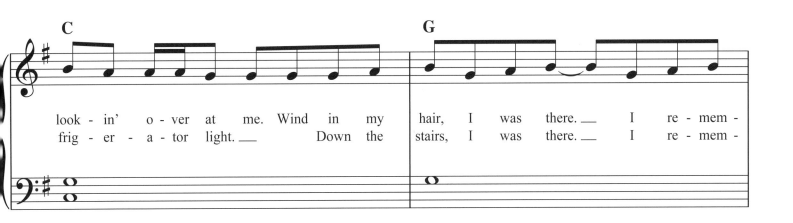

look - in' o - ver at me. Wind in my
frig - er - a - tor light. __ Down the

hair, I was there. __ I re - mem -
stairs, I was there. __ I re - mem -

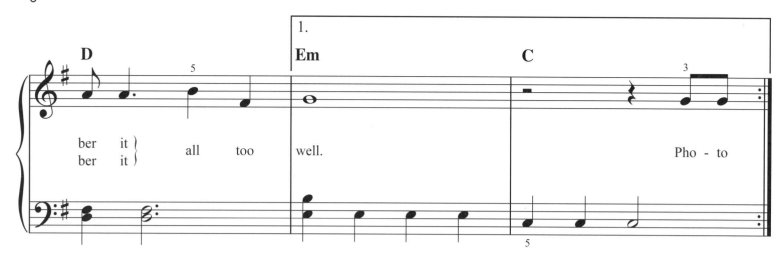

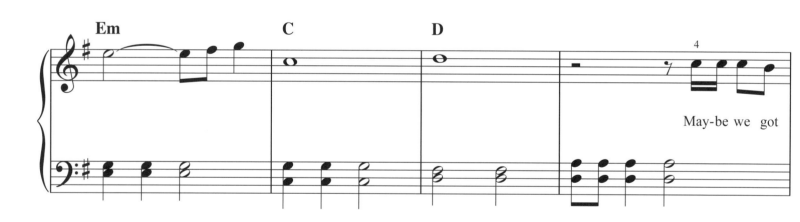

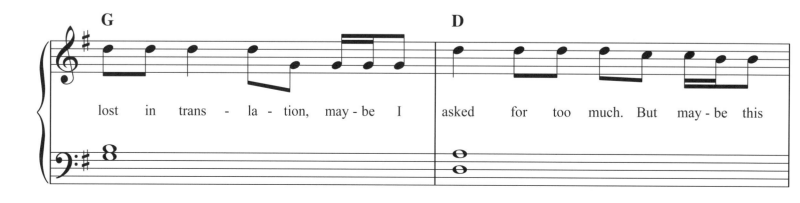

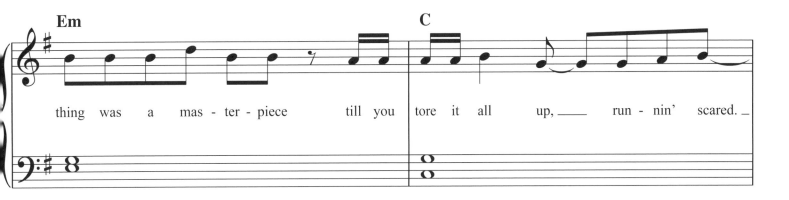

thing was a mas-ter-piece   till you   tore it all   up, ___ run-nin' scared. ___

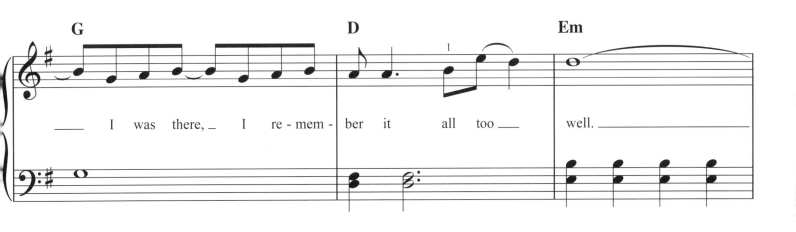

___ I was there, ___ I re-mem-ber it   all too ___   well. _____

___   And you   call me up ___ a-gain just to   break me like a prom-ise.   So

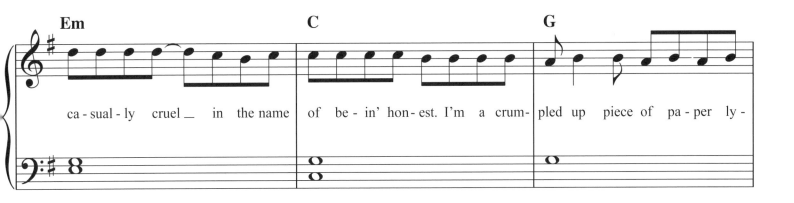

ca-sual-ly cruel ___ in the name   of be-in' hon-est. I'm a crum-pled up   piece of pa-per ly-

in' here 'cause I re-mem-ber it all, _____ all, _____ all _____

too well.

Time won't fly, it's like I'm par-a lyzed by it. I'd like to

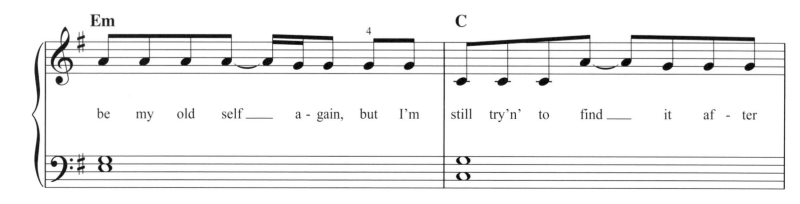

be my old self ____ a-gain, but I'm still try'n' to find ____ it af-ter

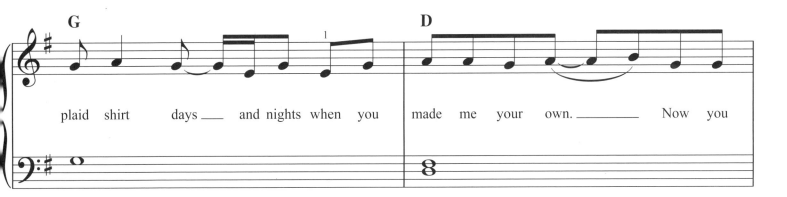

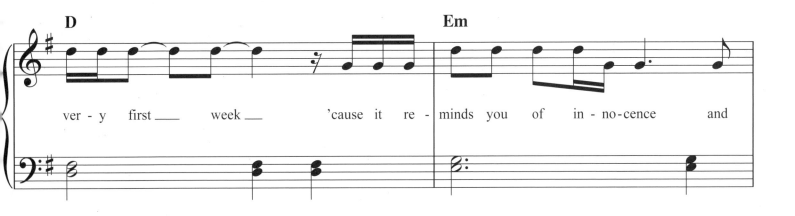

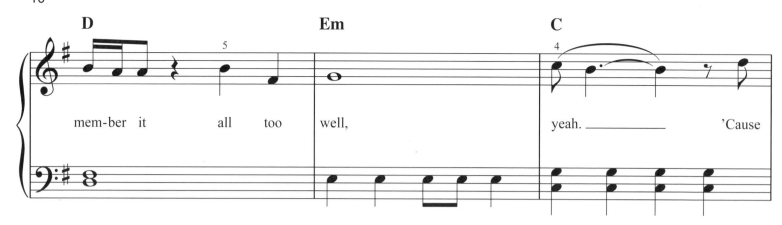

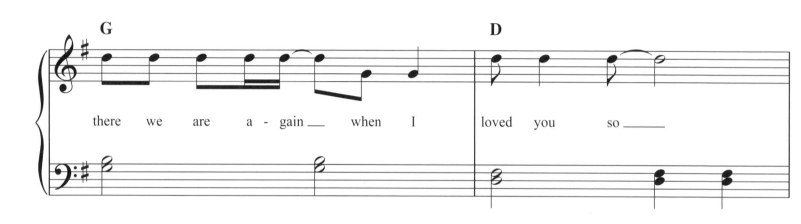

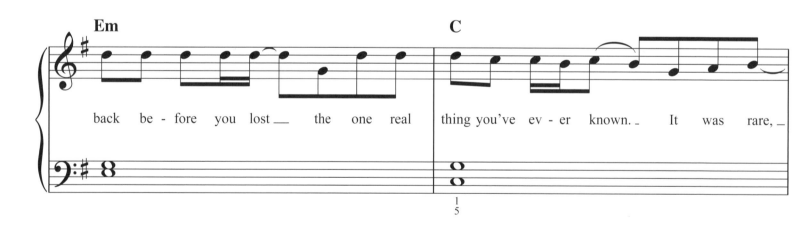

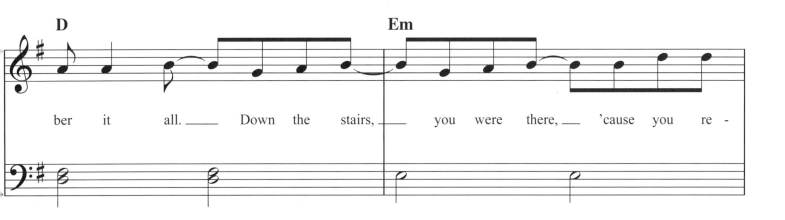

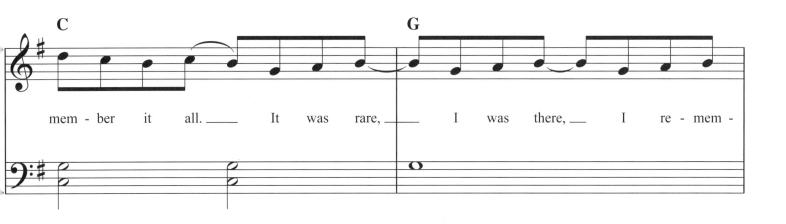

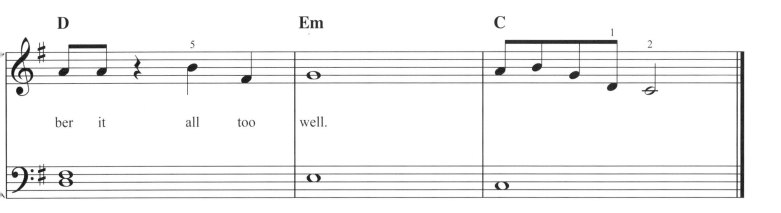

COLD HEART
(PNAU Remix)

Words and Music by ELTON JOHN,
BERNARD J.P. TAUPIN, NICHOLAS LITTLEMORE,
PETER MAYES, SAM LITTLEMORE,
DEAN MEREDITH and ANDREW JOHN MEECHAM

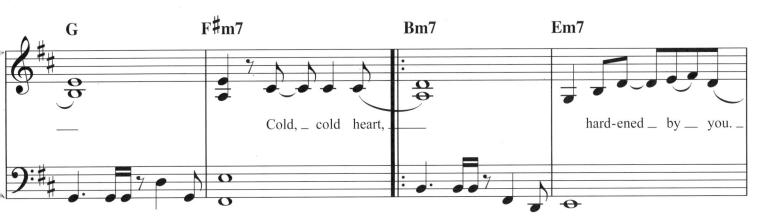

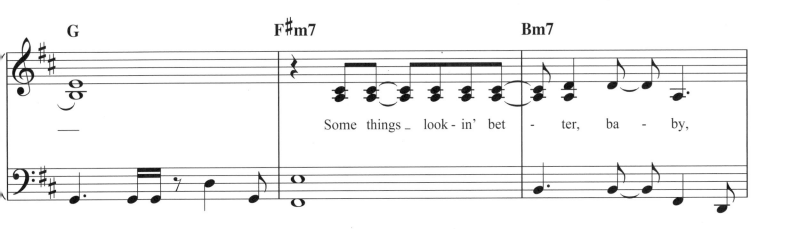

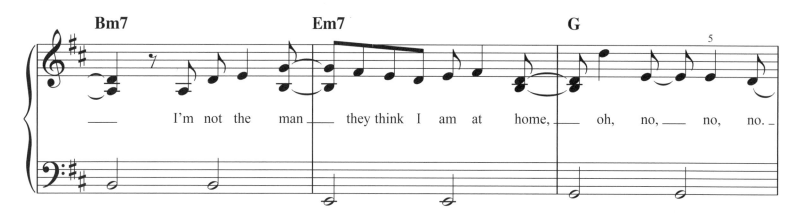

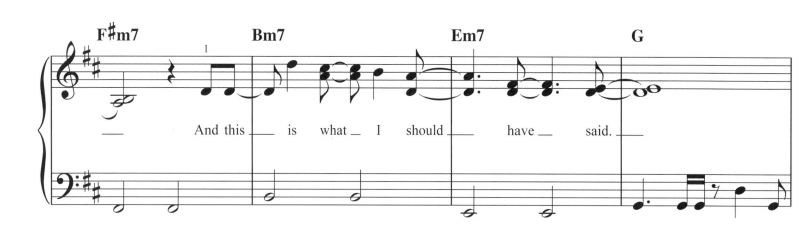

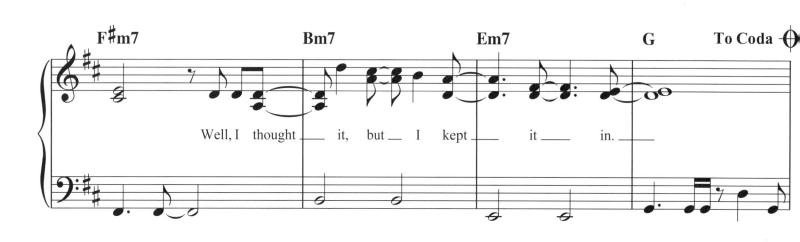

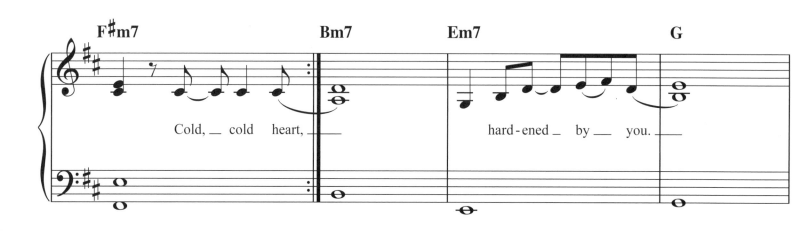

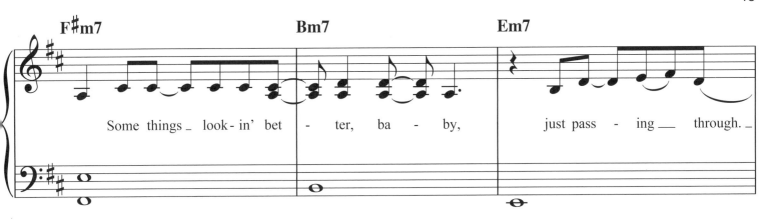

Some things _ look-in' bet - ter, ba - by, just pass - ing _ through. _

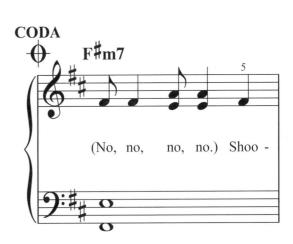

_ (Oh, no, no, no, no.) (No, no, no, no.) Shoo -

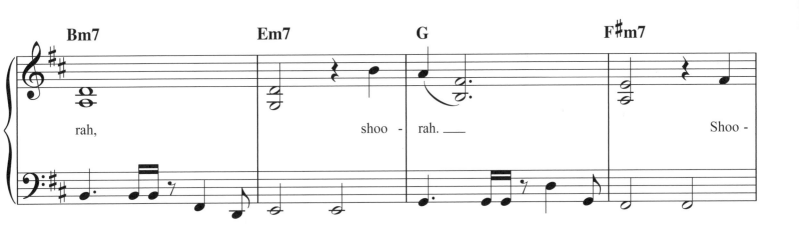

rah, shoo - rah. _ Shoo -

rah, shoo - rah. _ No, no, no, no.

FANCY LIKE

Words and Music by WALKER HAYES,
JOSH JENKINS, SHANE STEVENS
and CAMERON BARTOLINI

Moderately slow, in 2

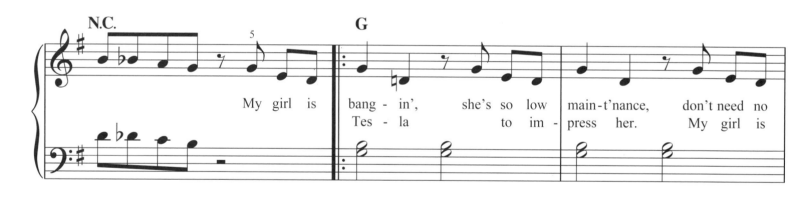

My girl is bang-in', she's so low main-t'nance, don't need no
Tes-la to im-press her. My girl is

cham-pagne pop-pin' en-ter-tain-ment. Take her to Wen-dy's, can't keep her
hap-py roll-in' on a Ves-pa. Don't need no man-sion to get ro-

off me. She wan-na / manc - in'. She's su - per

dip me like them fries in her Frost - y. / fine, __ dou - ble wide, slow __ danc - in'.

But

C

ev - 'ry now and then __ when I get paid, I got - ta

D

spoil __ my ba - by with an

up - grade, ay, ay, ay.

N.C.

Yeah, we fan - cy like

𝄋 G

Ap - ple - bee's on a

date night. Got that Bour - bon Street steak with the Or - e - o shake. Get some

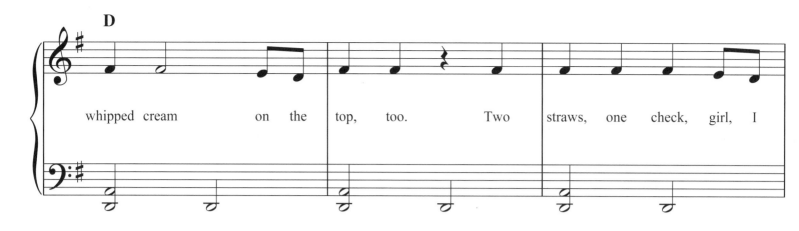

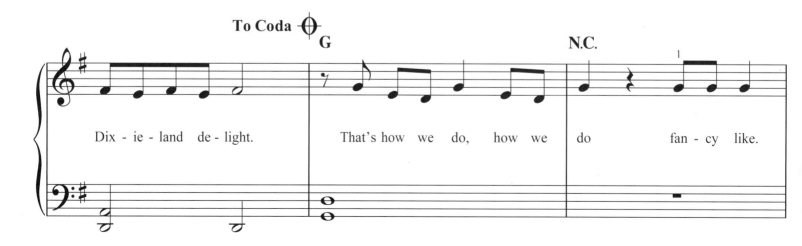

Yeah, she's prob-'ly gon' be keep-in' some Vic-tor-ia's Se-crets. May-be lit-tle May-bel-

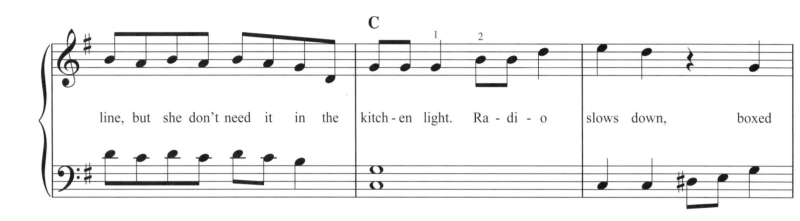

line, but she don't need it in the kitch-en light. Ra-di-o slows down, boxed

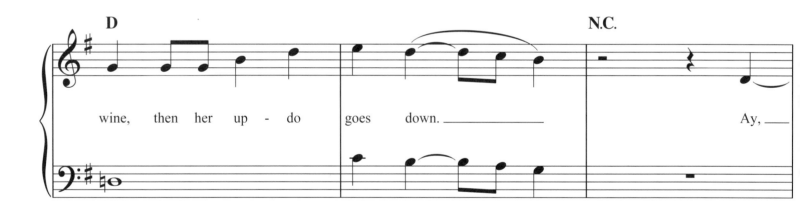

wine, then her up-do goes down. _____ Ay, _____

_____ yeah, we fan-cy like

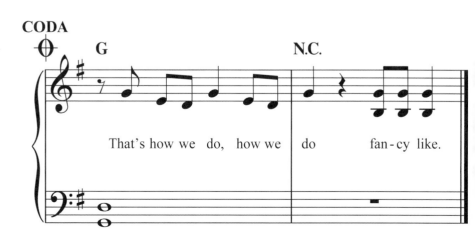

That's how we do, how we do fan-cy like.

EASY ON ME

Words and Music by ADELE ADKINS
and GREG KURSTIN

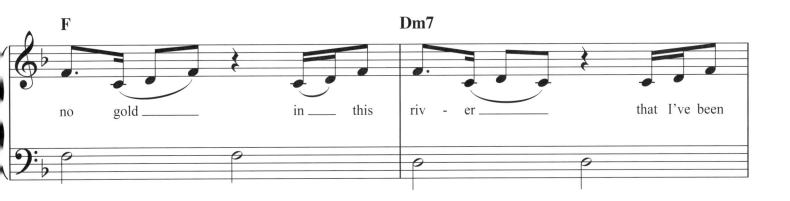

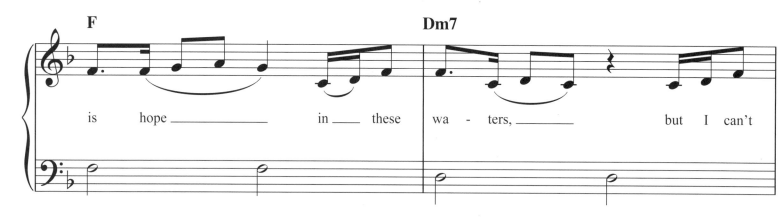

is hope _____ in ___ these wa - ters, _____ but I can't

bring my - self ___ to swim when I am ___ drown - ing in this

si - lence, __ ba - by. Let me in. _____ Go

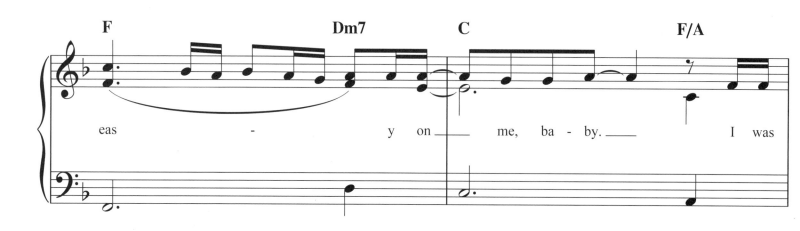

eas - y on ___ me, ba - by. ___ I was

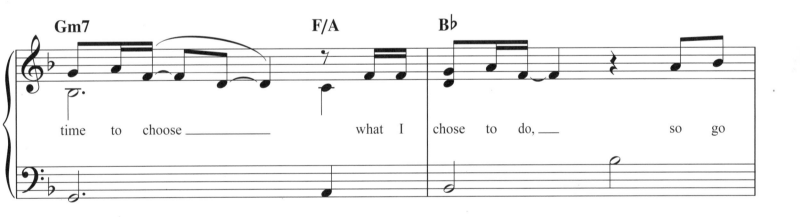

There __ ain't

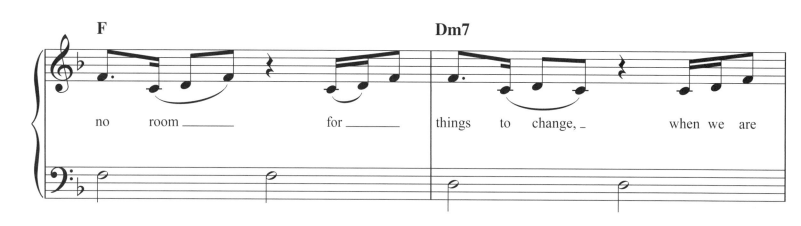

no room _____ for _____ | things to change, _ when we are

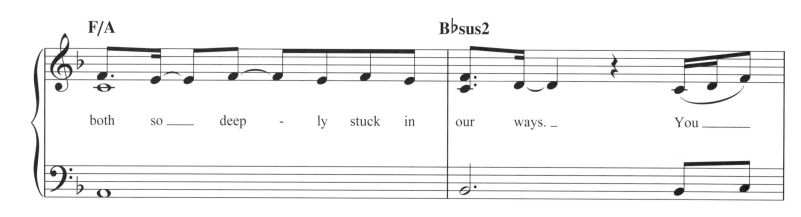

both so __ deep - ly stuck in | our ways. _ You _____

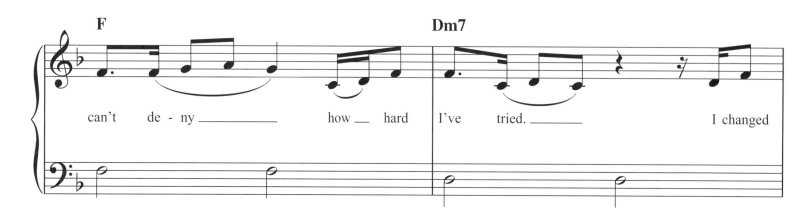

can't de - ny _____ how _ hard | I've tried. _____ I changed

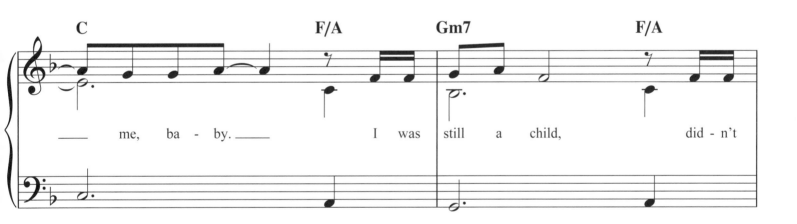

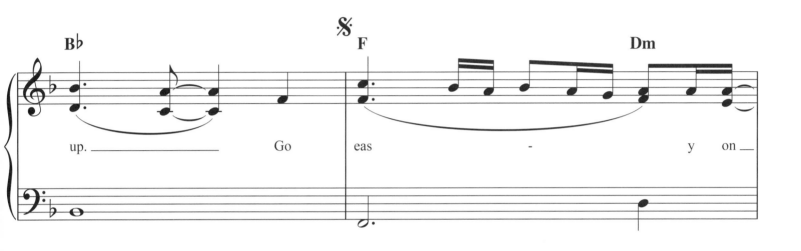

a - round me. I had no time to choose _____ what I

To Coda ⊕

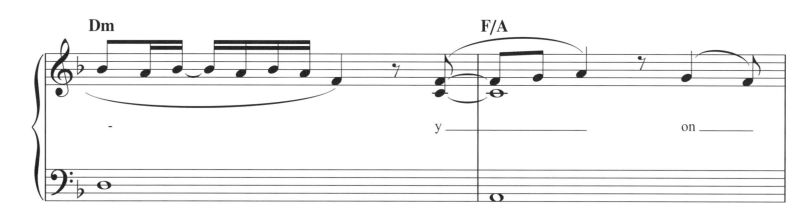

chose to do, ___ so go eas -

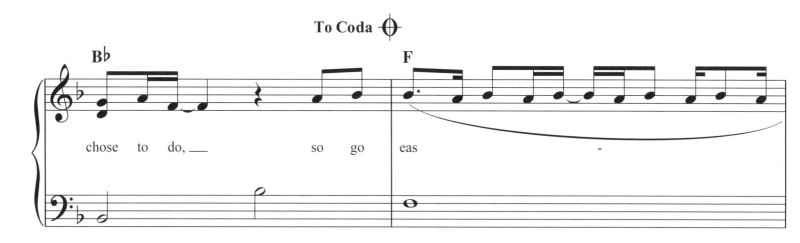

\- y _____ on _____

me. ___ I had ___ good in - ten - tions ___

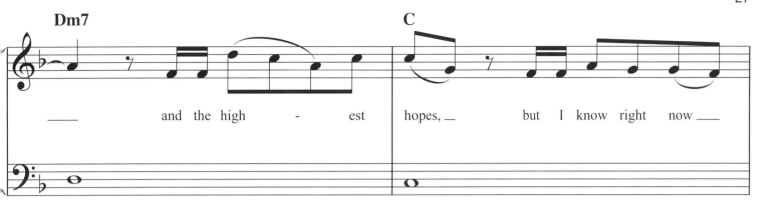

Dm7   **C**

and the high - est hopes, __ but I know right now __

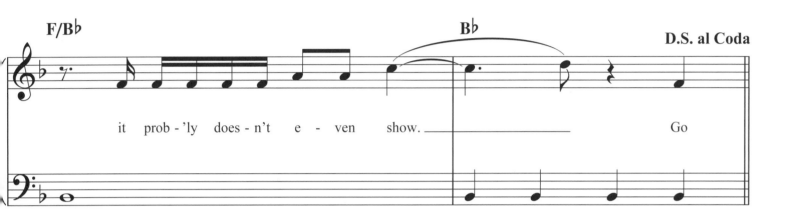

F/B♭   **B♭**   **D.S. al Coda**

it prob - 'ly does - n't e - ven show. _____ Go

CODA   **F**   **Dm7**

eas - y ____ on me.

F/A   **B♭**

GHOST

Words and Music by JUSTIN BIEBER,
JONATHAN BELLION, JORDAN JOHNSON,
STEFAN JOHNSON and MICHAEL POLLACK

Young blood thinks there's al - ways to - mor - row.
Young blood thinks there's al - ways to - mor - row.

I miss your touch on nights ___
Need more time, but time ___

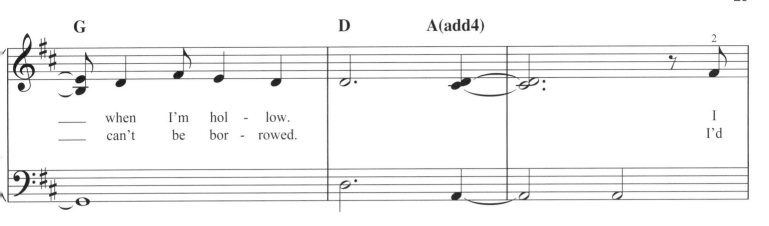

G   D   A(add4)

_____ when I'm hol - low.
_____ can't be bor - rowed.   I   I'd

Bm   G   D   A(add4)

know you crossed a bridge that   I can't fol - low. _____
leave it all be - hind if   I could fol - low. _____

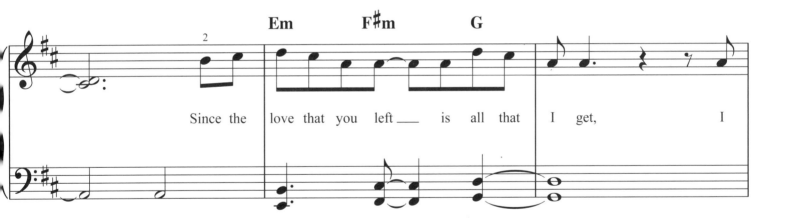

Em   F♯m   G

Since the love that you left ___ is all that I get,   I

Bm   A   Bm   G

want you to know ___ that if I can't be close ___ to you

I'll set-tle for the ghost of you. I miss you

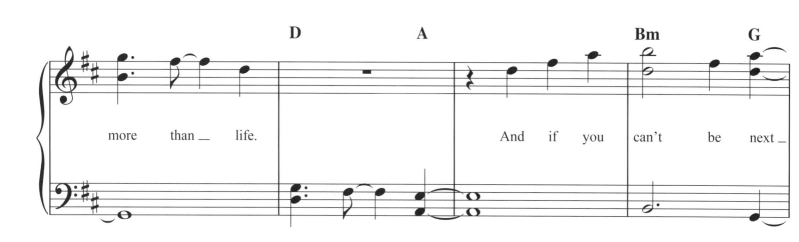

more than ___ life. And if you can't be next ___

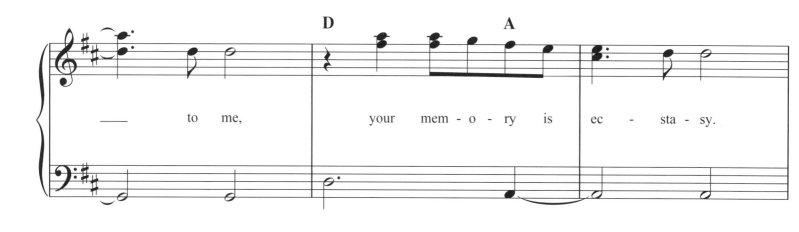

___ to me, your mem-o-ry is ec-sta-sy.

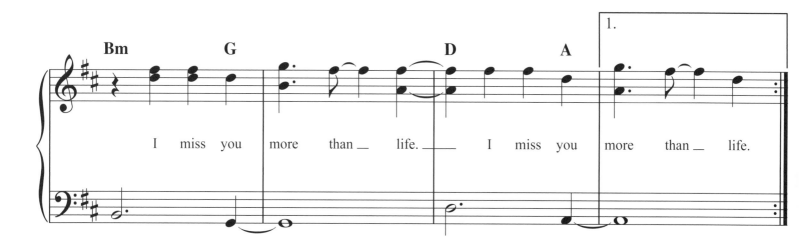

1.

I miss you more than ___ life. ___ I miss you more than ___ life.

I miss you more than ___ life.

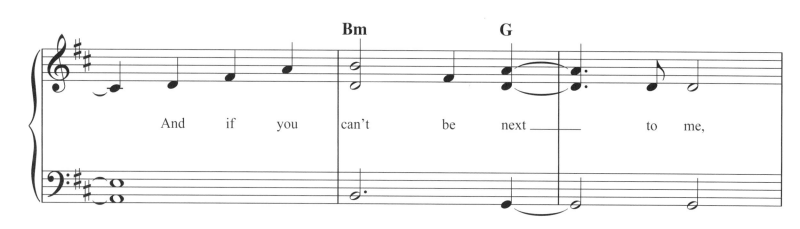

And if you can't be next ___ to me,

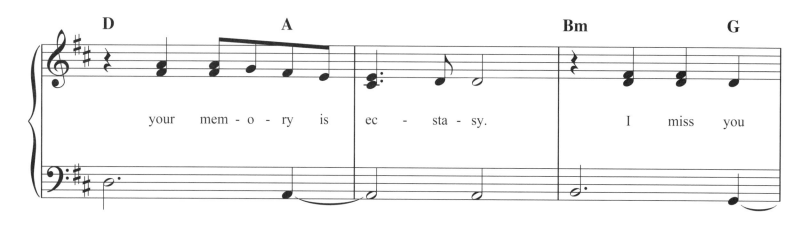

your mem-o-ry is ec-sta-sy. I miss you

more than ___ life. ___ I miss you more than ___ life.

FOLLOW YOU

Words and Music by DAN REYNOLDS,
WAYNE SERMON, BEN McKEE,
DANIEL PLATZMAN, ELLEY DUHÉ,
JOEL LITTLE and FRANSICSA HALL

Moderately fast

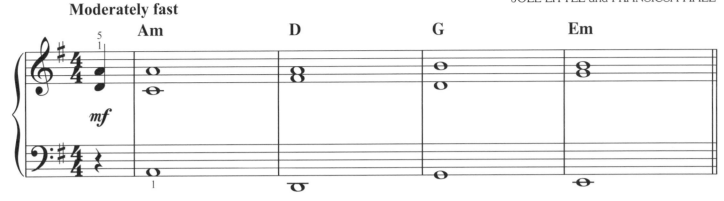

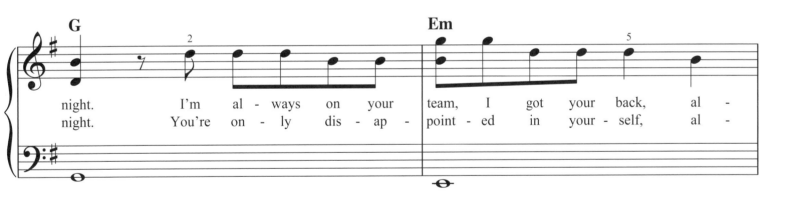

You know I / Call you up, got your num - ber, num - ber all ___
you've been cry - in', cry - in' all ___

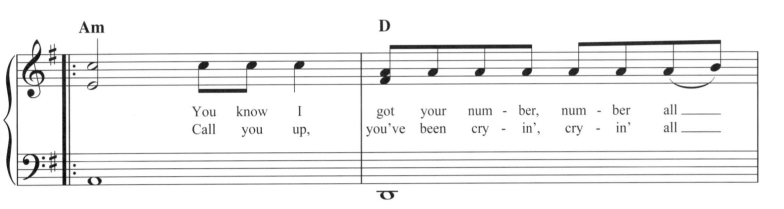

night. I'm al - ways on your team, I got your back, al -
night. You're on - ly dis - ap - point - ed in your - self, al -

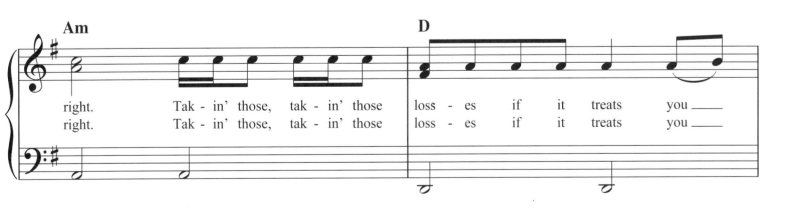

right. Tak - in' those, tak - in' those loss - es if it treats you ___
right. Tak - in' those, tak - in' those loss - es if it treats you ___

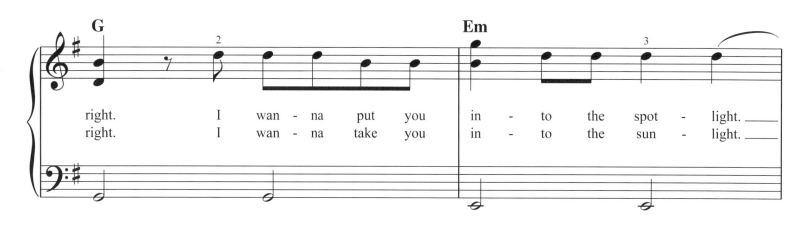

right.   I   wan - na   put   you   in - to   the   spot - light. ____
right.   I   wan - na   take   you   in - to   the   sun - light. ____

_____   If   the   world   would   on - ly   know   what   you've   been   hold - in'   back,

heart   at - tacks   ev - 'ry   night.   Oh,   you   know   it's   not   right.   I   will   fol - low   you   way

down   wher - ev - er   you   may   go.   I'll   fol - low   you   way   down   to   your   deep - est

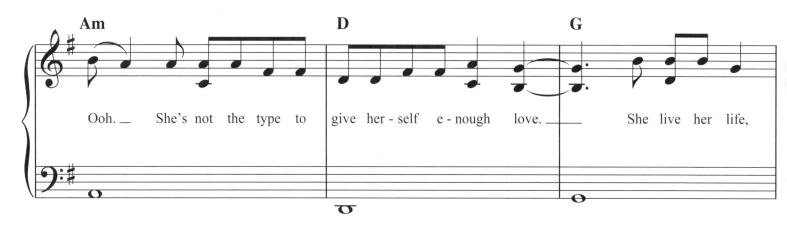

Ooh.__ She's not the type to give her-self e-nough love.__ She live her life,

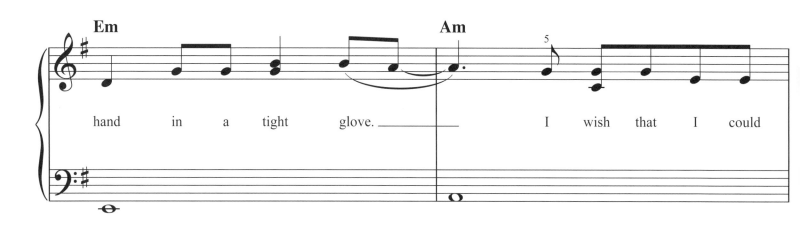

hand in a tight glove.__ I wish that I could

fix it, I could fix it for you.__ But in-stead, I'll be right here com-in' through.

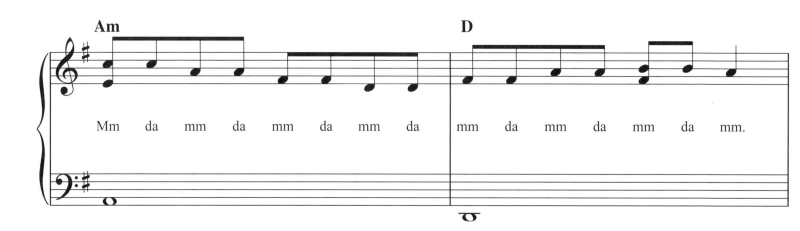

Mm da mm da mm da mm da mm da mm da mm da mm.

Mm da mm da mm da mm. Right here com - in' through.

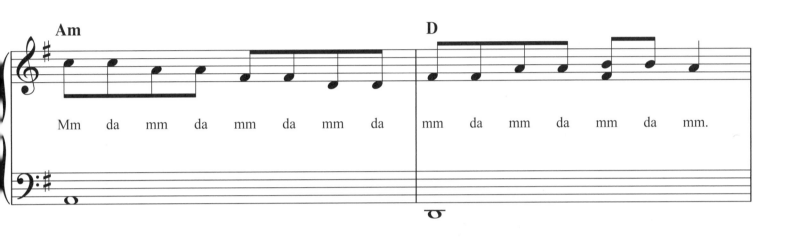

Mm da mm da mm da mm da mm da mm da mm da mm.

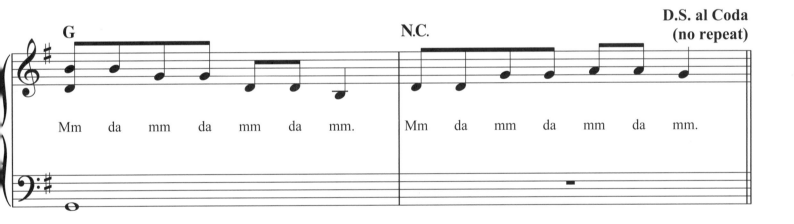

Mm da mm da mm da mm. Mm da mm da mm da mm.

D.S. al Coda
(no repeat)

CODA

Ooh.

HAPPIER THAN EVER

Words and Music by BILLIE EILISH O'CONNELL
and FINNEAS O'CONNELL

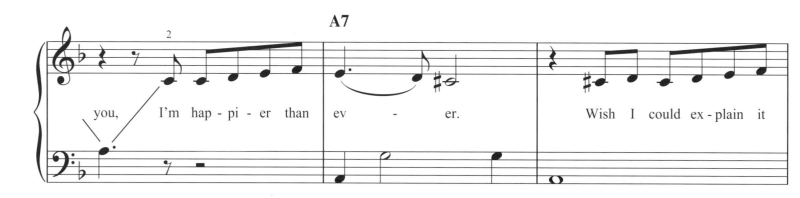

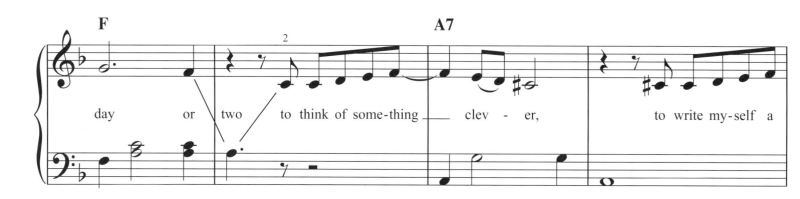

let - ter to tell me what to do. _____

_____ Do you read my in - ter-views or _____

do you skip my av - e -nue? When you said you were pass-in' through, was I

e - ven on your way? I _____ knew when I asked you to be

cool a - bout what I was tell - ing you, you would do the op - po - site of what you

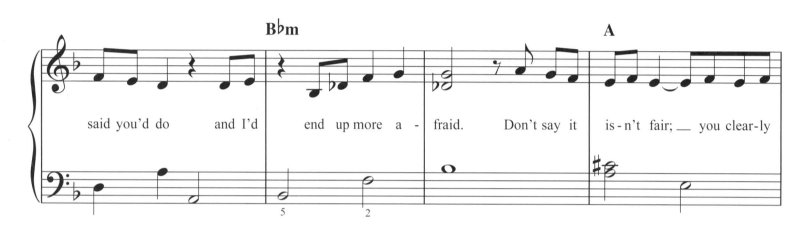

said you'd do and I'd end up more a - fraid. Don't say it is - n't fair; — you clear - ly

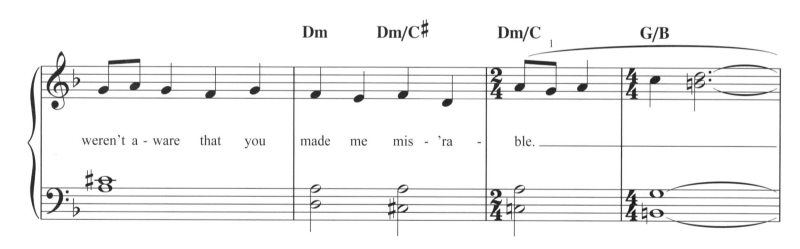

weren't a - ware that you made me mis - 'ra - ble. ____

— So, if you real - ly wan - na know, when I'm a - way from

A7   Dm

you, I'm hap-pi-er than ev - er. Wish I could ex-plain it bet -

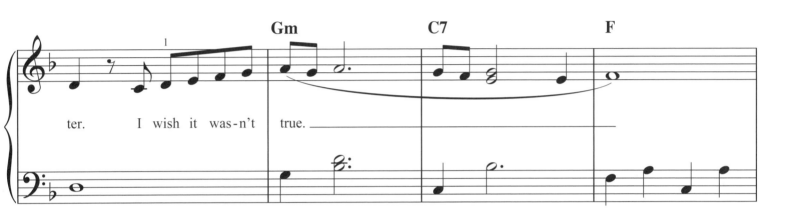

Gm   C7   F

ter. I wish it was-n't true.

Moderate Waltz, in 2

C   F   Am   Dm

B♭   B♭m   F   Am

You call me a - gain, drunk in your Benz.

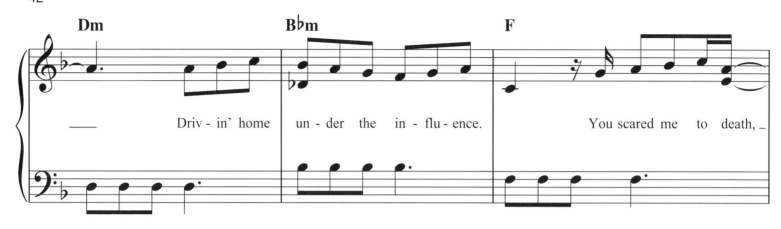

Driv-in' home un-der the in-flu-ence. You scared me to death,

but I'm wast-in' my breath 'cause you on-ly lis-ten to your

friends.
I don't re-late to you. I don't re-late to you,

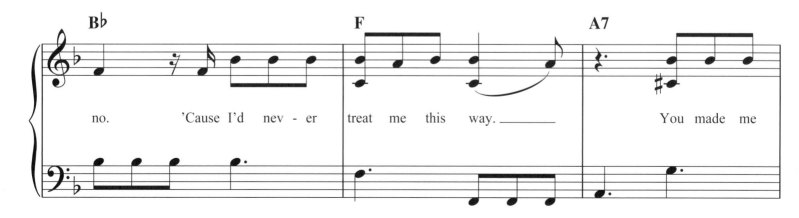

no. 'Cause I'd nev-er treat me this way. You made me

hate this cit - y.   And I don't talk   bad a-bout you on the

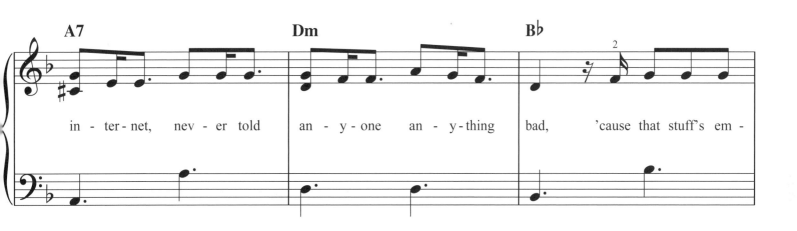

in - ter-net,   nev-er told   an - y -one   an - y -thing   bad,   'cause that stuff's em -

bar - rass-ing.   You were my   ev -'ry -thing and all   that you   did was make me _____

sad.   So   don't waste the time __ I don't   have   and

don't try to make me feel bad. I could talk a-bout ev-'ry time that you showed

up on time, but I'd have an emp - ty line 'cause you nev-er did. Nev-er paid an-y mind

to my moth-er or friends, so I shut 'em all out for you 'cause I was a kid.

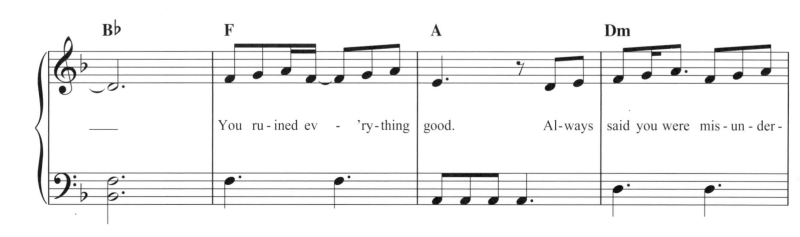

You ru-ined ev-'ry-thing good. Al-ways said you were mis-un-der-

stood.　　Made all　my　mo - ments your　own.

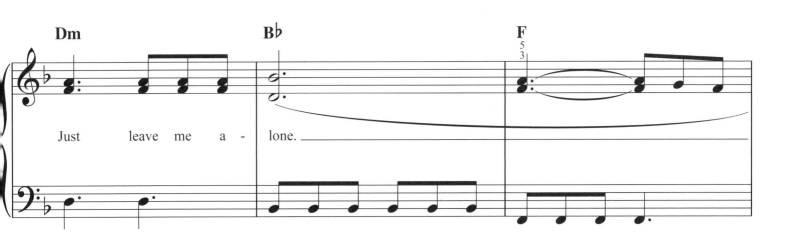

Just　leave me a -　lone. _____

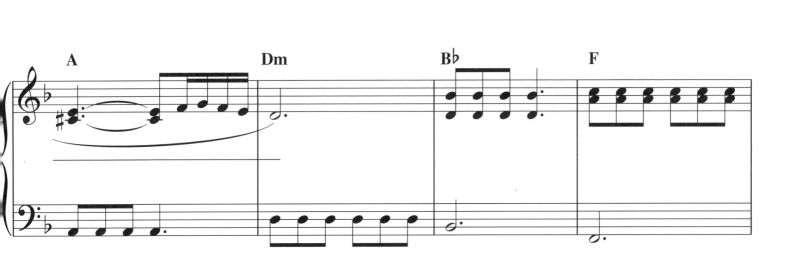

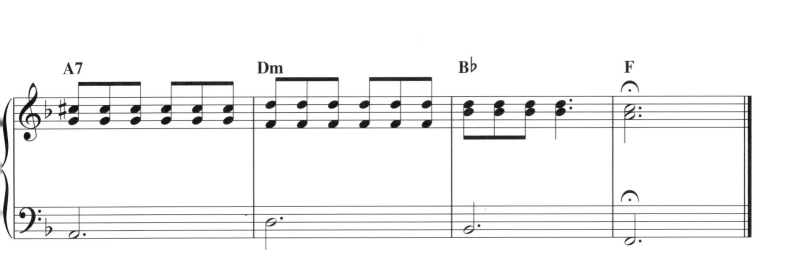

HEAT WAVES

Words and Music by
DAVE BAYLEY

Moderate Pop

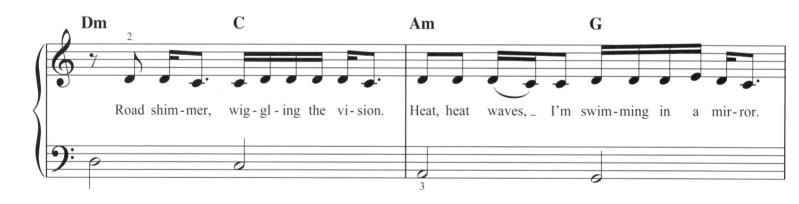

Road shim-mer, wig-gl-ing the vi-sion. Heat, heat waves, _ I'm swim-ming in a mir-ror.

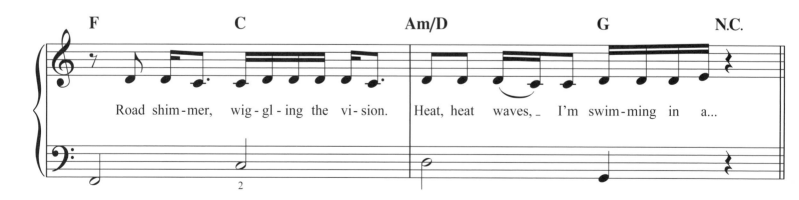

Road shim-mer, wig-gl-ing the vi-sion. Heat, heat waves, _ I'm swim-ming in a...

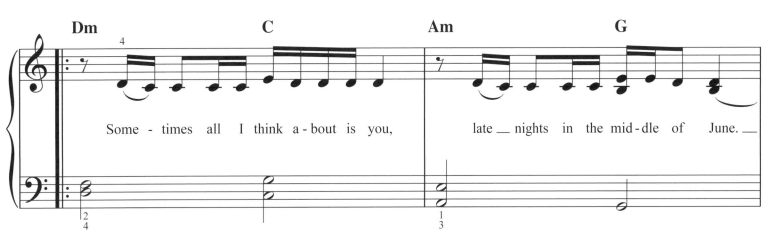

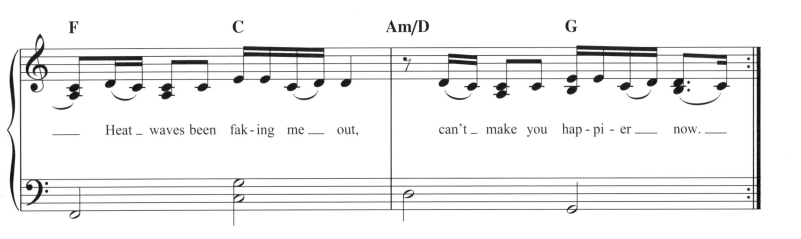

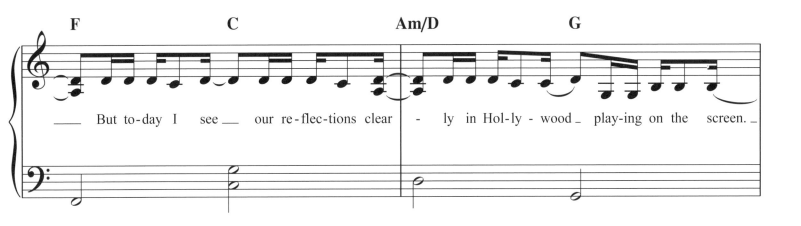

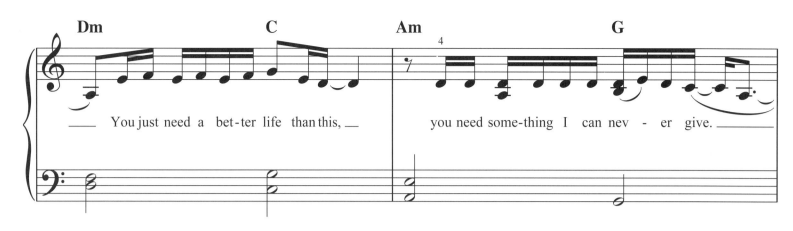

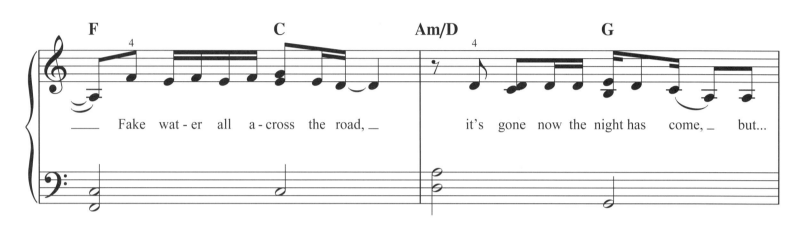

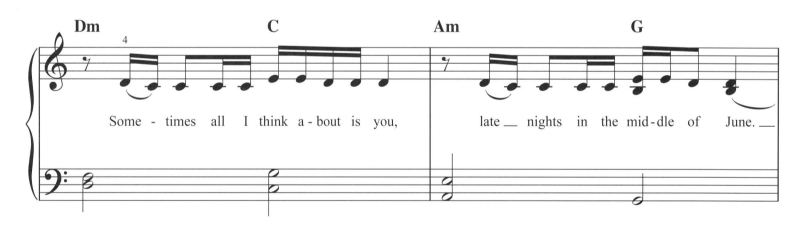

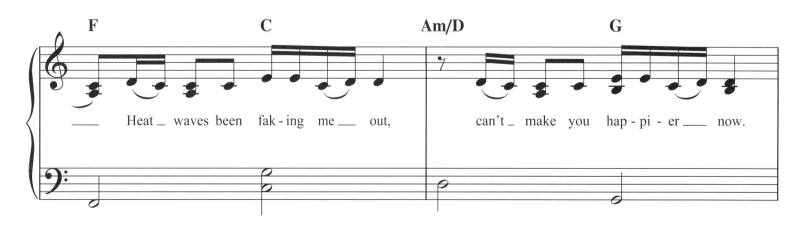

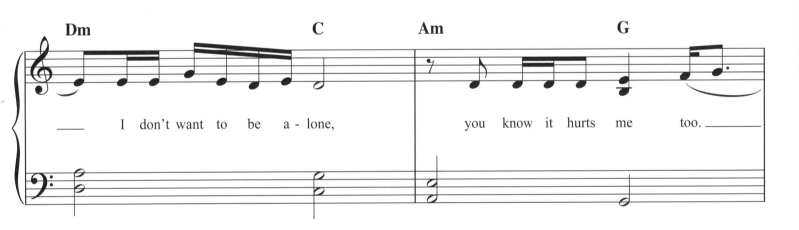

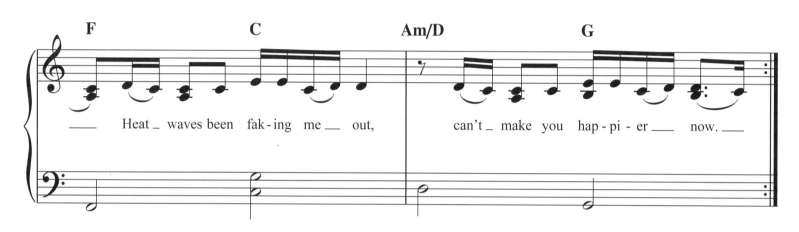

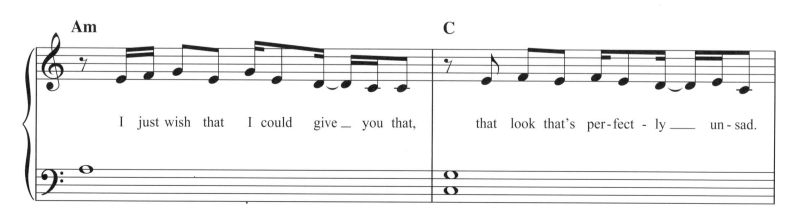

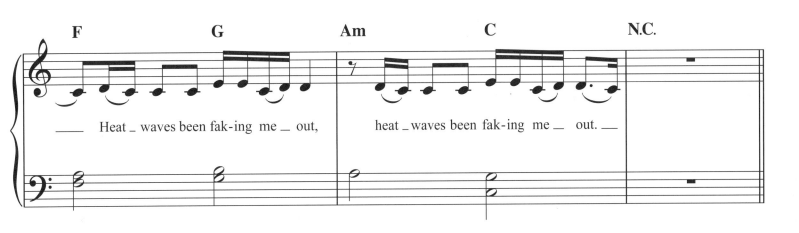

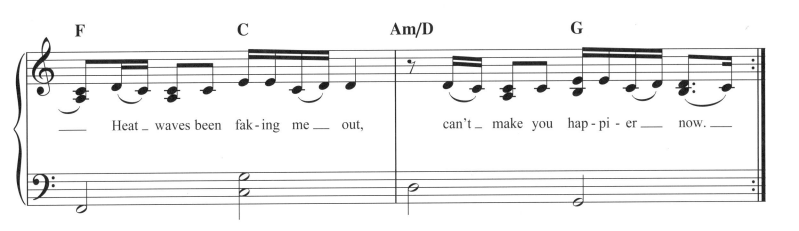

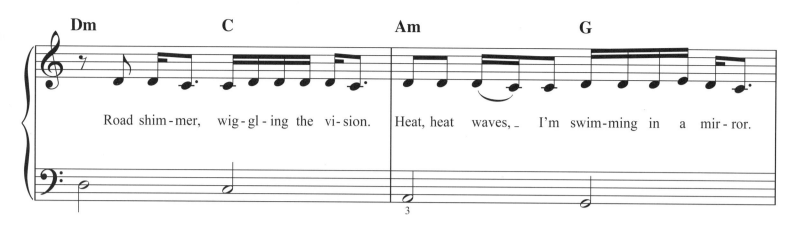

Road shim-mer, wig-gl-ing the vi-sion. Heat, heat waves,_ I'm swim-ming in a mir-ror.

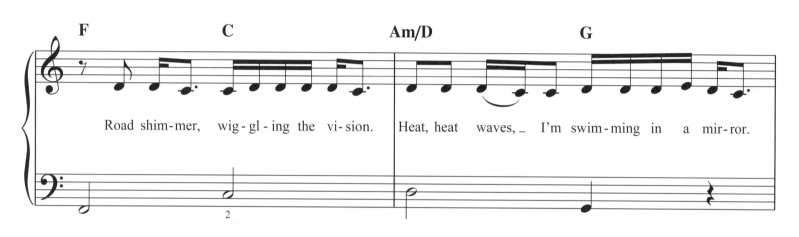

Road shim-mer, wig-gl-ing the vi-sion. Heat, heat waves,_ I'm swim-ming in a mir-ror.

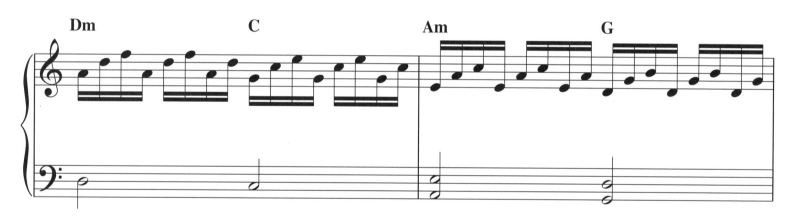

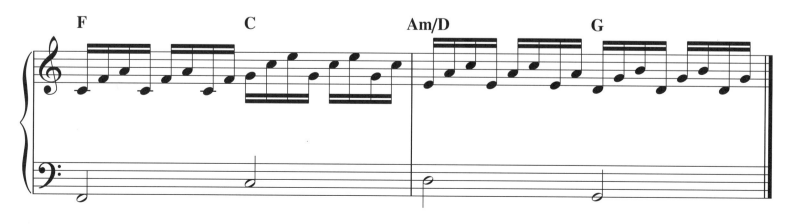

IT'LL BE OKAY

Words and Music by SHAWN MENDES,
SCOTT HARRIS, MICHAEL SABATH
and EDDIE BENJAMIN

Moderately slow

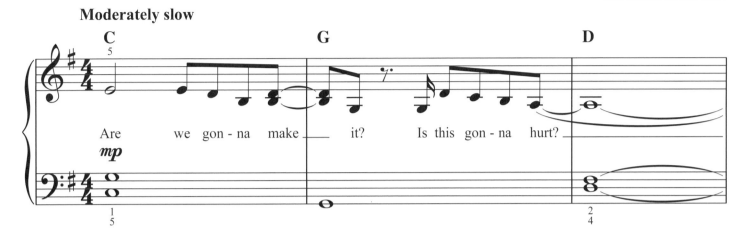

Are we gon - na make it? Is this gon - na hurt?

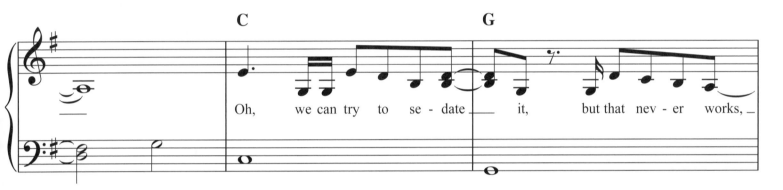

Oh, we can try to se - date it, but that nev - er works,

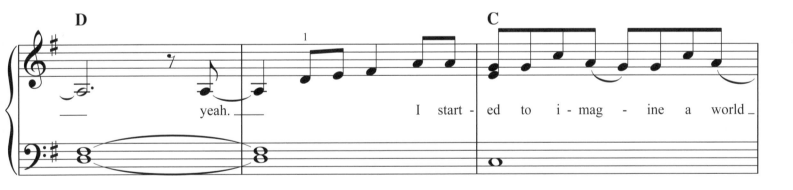

yeah. I start - ed to i - mag - ine a world

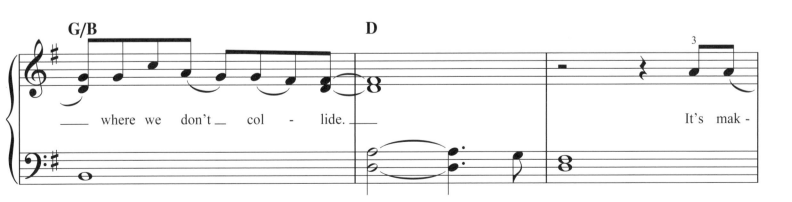

where we don't col - lide. It's mak -

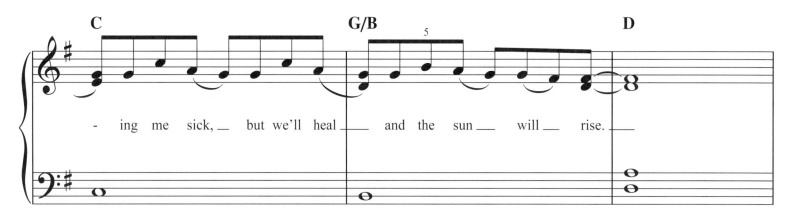

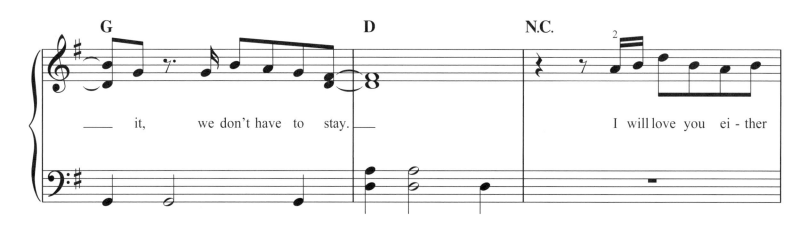

way, ooh, _____ it-'ll be oh, be o-

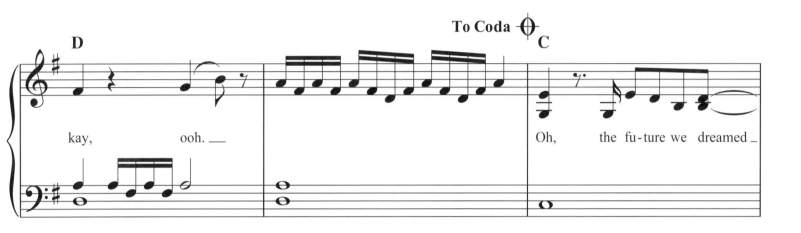

kay, ooh. _____ Oh, the fu-ture we dreamed _

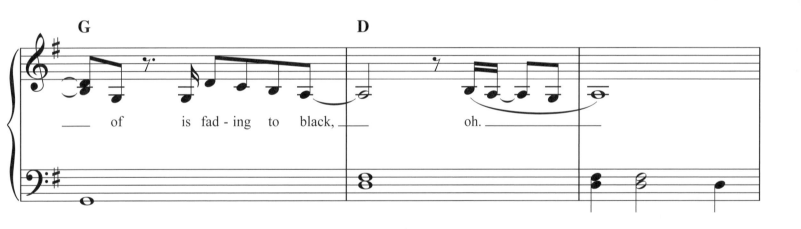

_____ of is fad-ing to black, _____ oh. _____

Oh, there's noth-ing more pain - ful, noth-ing more pain - ful, _____ oh. _

56

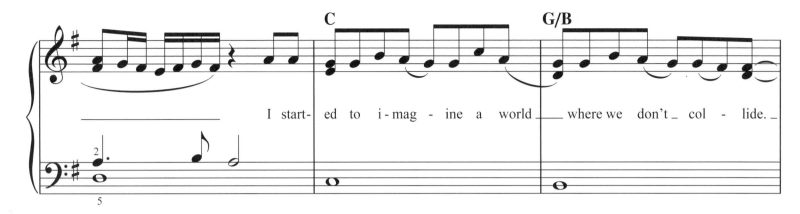

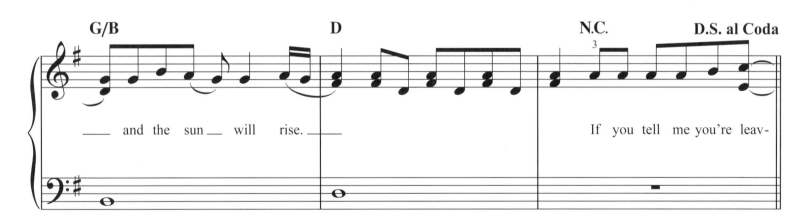

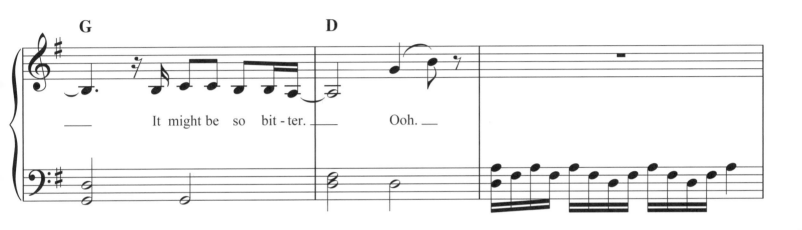

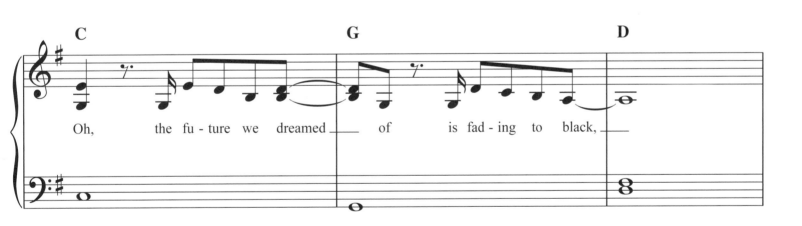

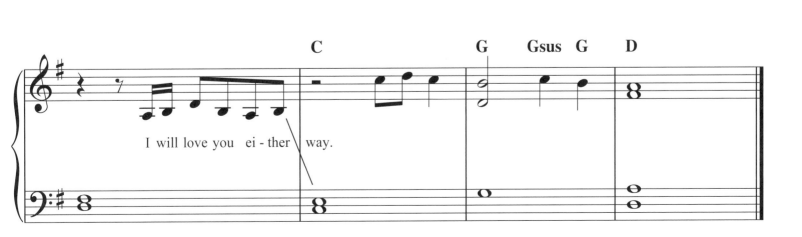

IF I DIDN'T LOVE YOU

Words and Music by KURT ALLISON,
TULLY KENNEDY, JOHN MORGAN
and LYDIA VAUGHAN

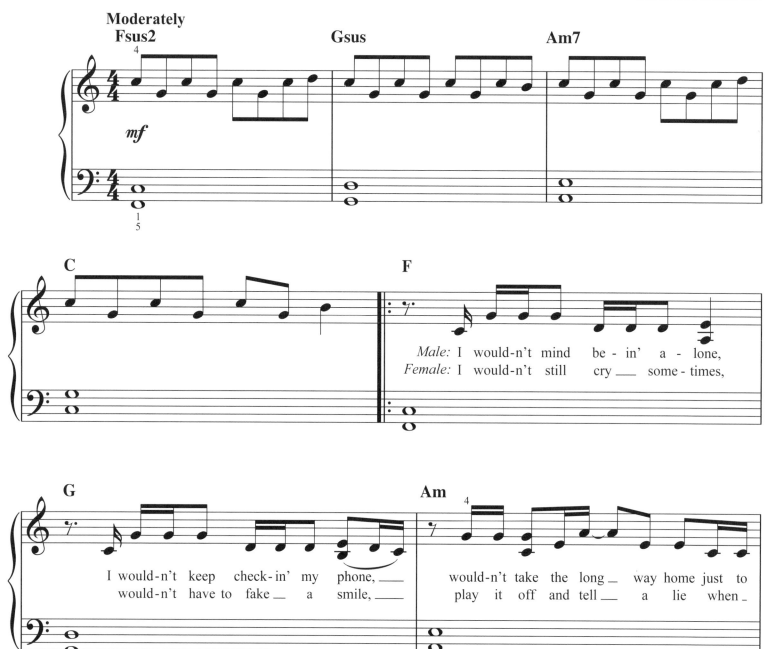

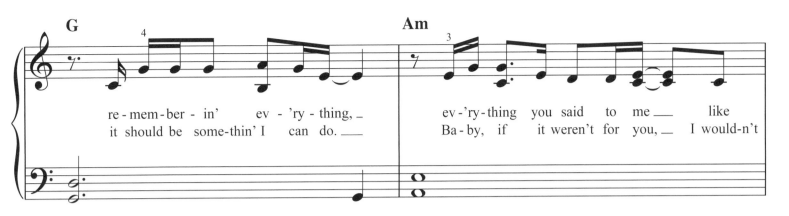

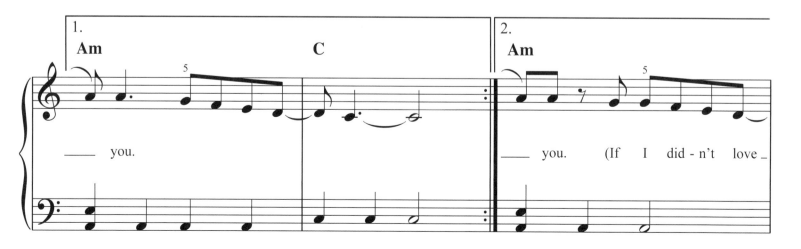

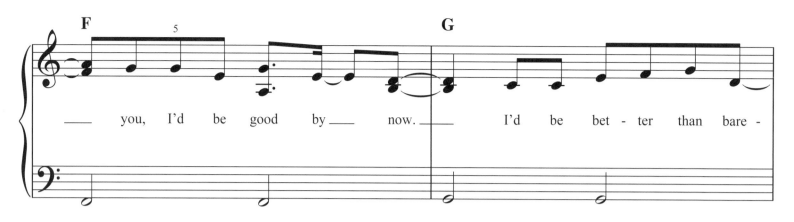

you, I'd be good by ___ now. ___ I'd be bet-ter than bare-

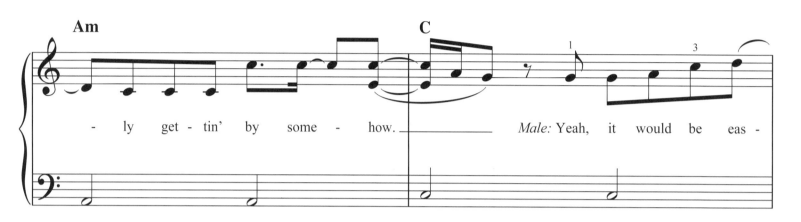

- ly get-tin' by some-how. _____ *Male:* Yeah, it would be eas-

- y not to miss you, won-der a-bout who's with you, turn the

"want you" off when-ev-er I want ___ to. If I did-n't love ___ you, ___

if I did - n't love ____ you. ____ (If I did - n't love ____

____ you.) If I did - n't love ____ you. (If I did - n't love ____

Both:
____ you.) If I did - n't love ____ you.

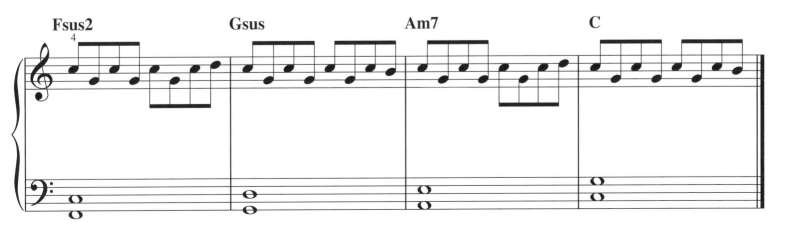

LOVE AGAIN

Words and Music by DUA LIPA,
CLARENCE BERNARD COFFEE, CHELCEE GRIMES,
STEPHEN KOZMENIUK, BING CROSBY,
IRVING WALLMAN and MAX WARTELL

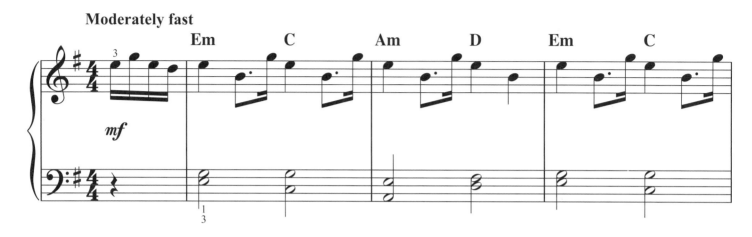

I nev-er thought that I would find a way out. ___
I used to think that I was made out of stone. ___
So man-y nights my tears fell hard-er than rain, ___

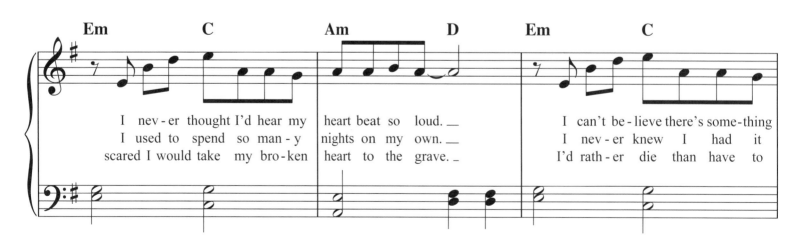

I nev-er thought I'd hear my heart beat so loud. ___ I can't be-lieve there's some-thing
I used to spend so man-y nights on my own. ___ I nev-er knew I had it
scared I would take my bro-ken heart to the grave. ___ I'd rath-er die than have to

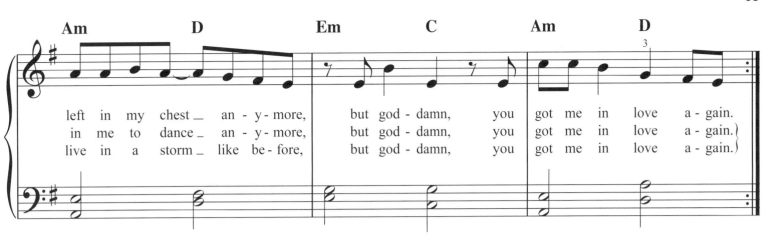

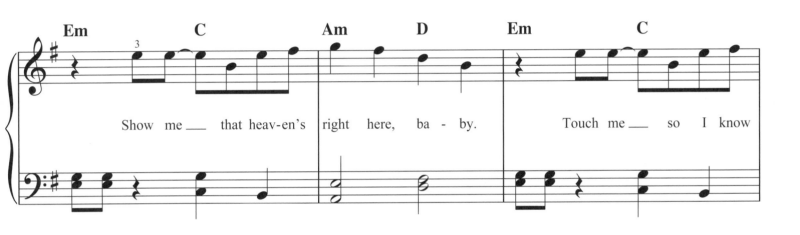

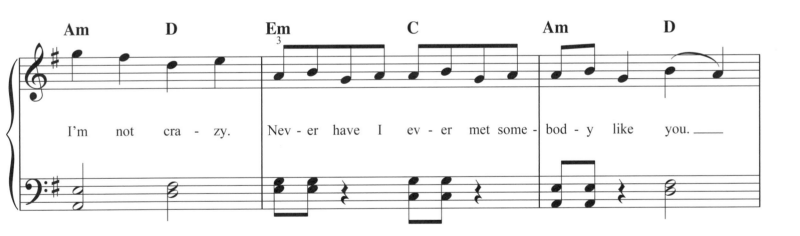

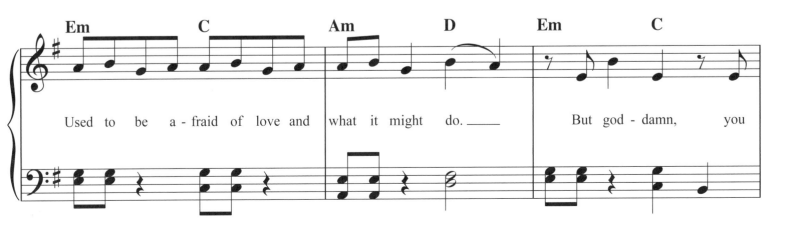

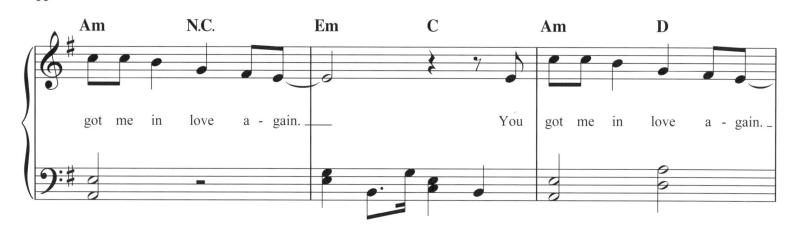

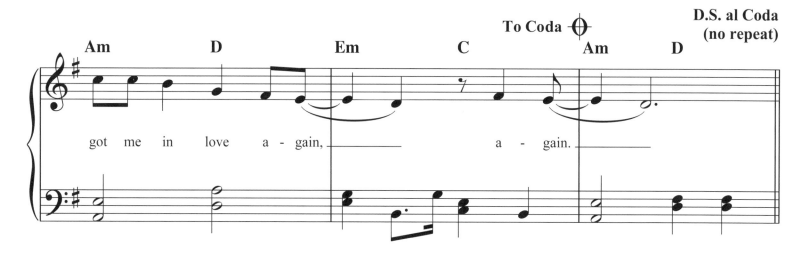

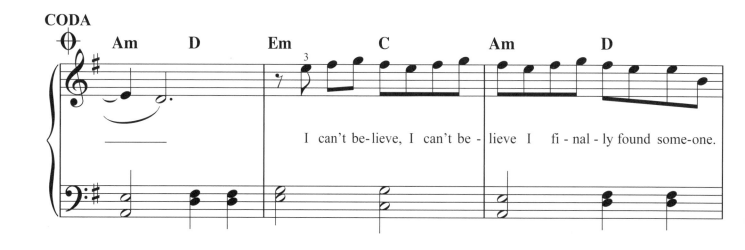

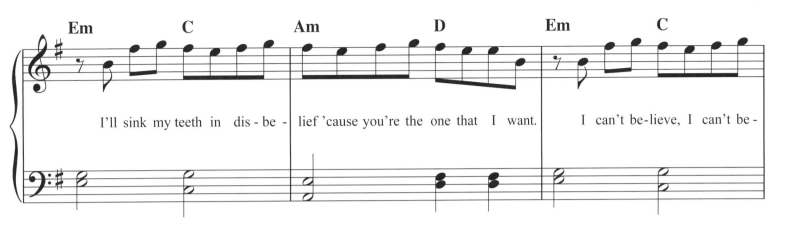

I'll sink my teeth in dis - be - lief 'cause you're the one that I want. I can't be-lieve, I can't be-

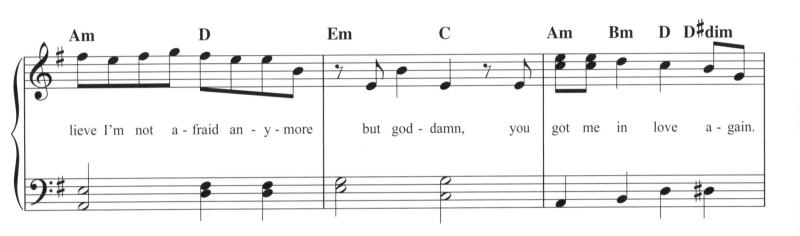

lieve I'm not a - fraid an - y - more but god - damn, you got me in love a - gain.

I nev - er thought that I would

find a way out. ___ I nev - er thought I'd hear my heart beat so loud. ___

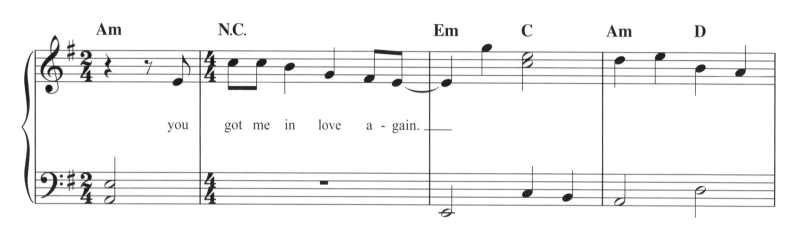

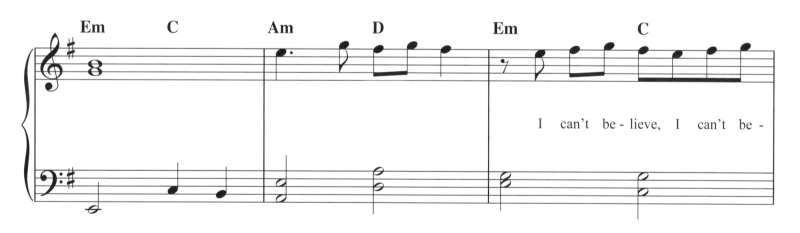

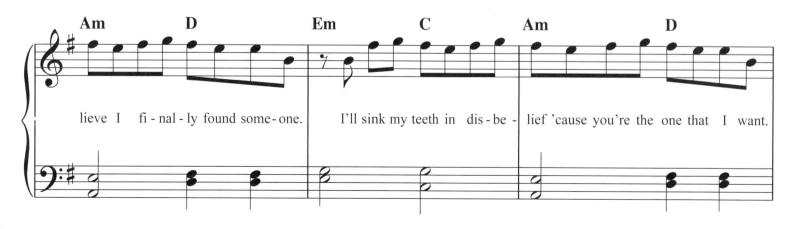

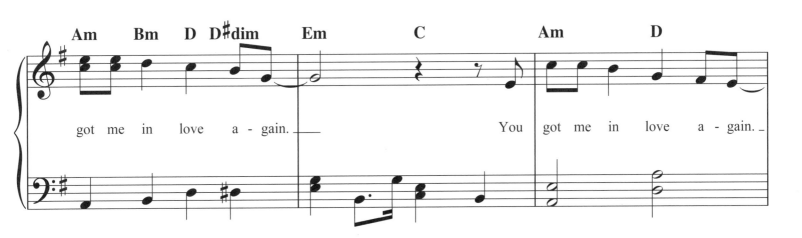

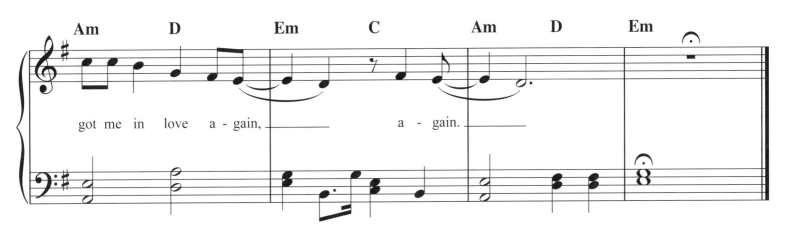

MY UNIVERSE

Words and Music by CHRIS MARTIN,
WILL CHAMPION, JON BUCKLAND,
GUY BERRYMAN, MAX MARTIN,
HO-SEOK JUNG, NAM-JOON KIM,
YOON-GI MIN, OSCAR HOLTER
and BILL RAHKO

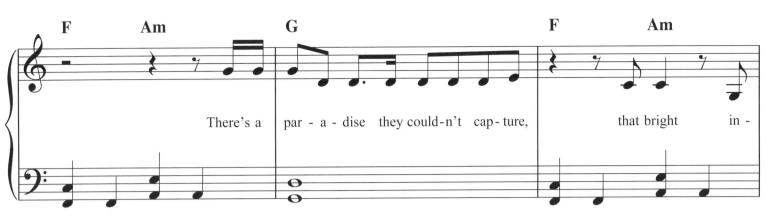

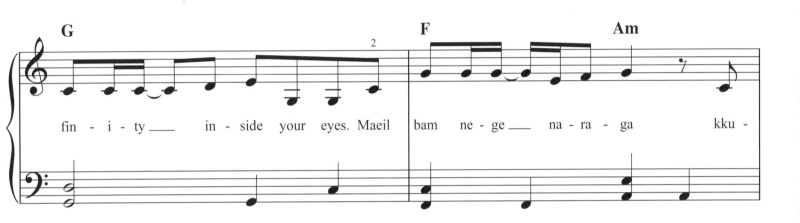

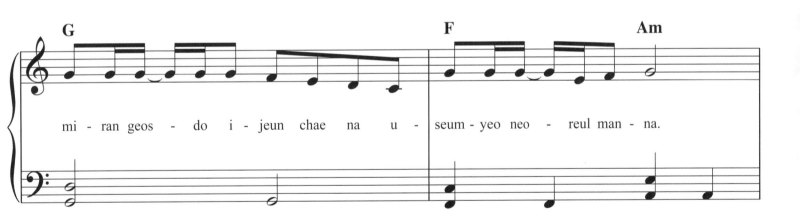

I just want to put you first. _____ And you, you are my

u – ni – verse _ and you make my world light up in – side. _____

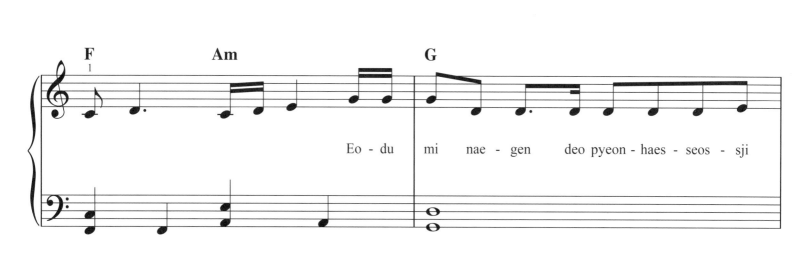

Eo – du mi nae – gen deo pyeon – haes – seos – sji

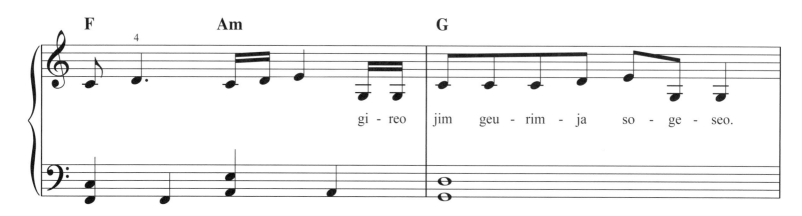

gi – reo jim geu – rim – ja so – ge – seo.

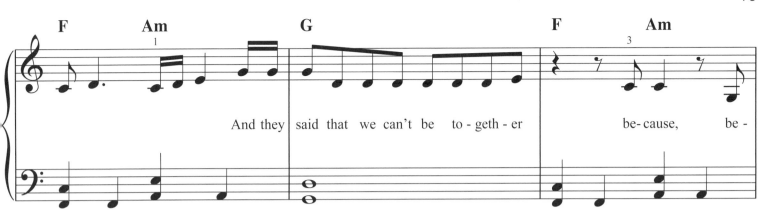

And they said that we can't be to - geth - er   be - cause,   be -

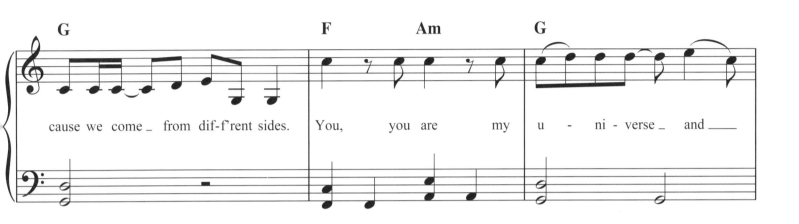

cause we come _ from dif - f'rent sides.   You,   you   are   my   u   -   ni - verse _ and ____

I   just want   to   put you   first. _____   And   you,   you   are   my

u   -   ni - verse _ and   you make my world light up   in - side. ____   My u - ni - verse. _

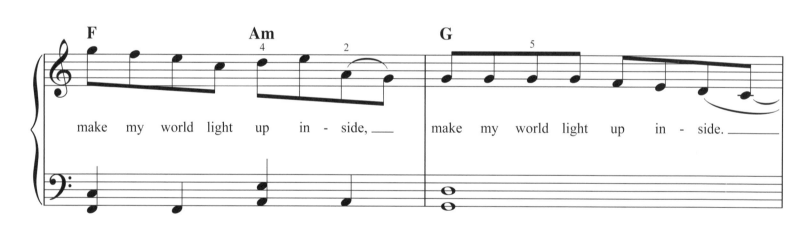

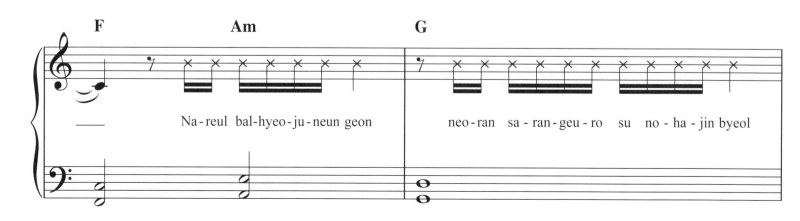

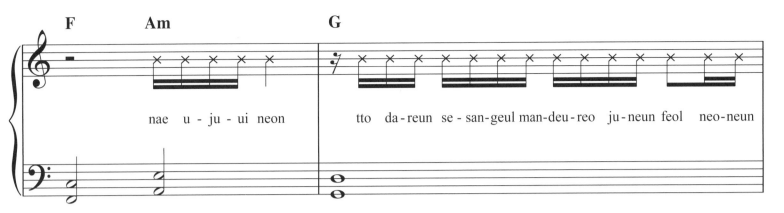

nae u - ju - ui neon
tto da - reun se - san-geul man-deu - reo ju - neun feol neo-neun

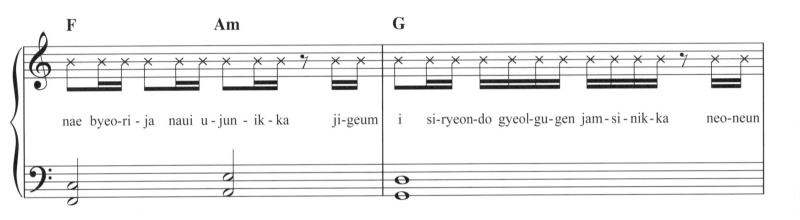

nae byeo-ri - ja naui u - jun - ik - ka ji-geum i si-ryeon-do gyeol-gu-gen jam-si - nik - ka neo-neun

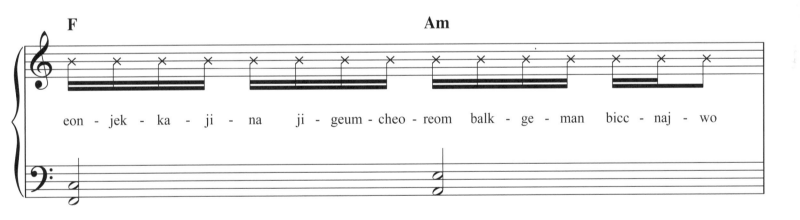

eon - jek - ka - ji - na ji - geum - cheo - reom balk - ge - man bicc - naj - wo

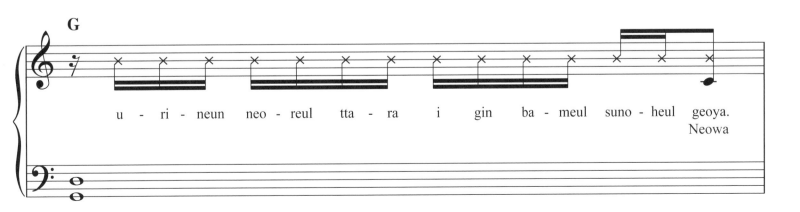

u - ri - neun neo - reul tta - ra i gin ba - meul suno-heul geoya.
Neowa

hamk - ke ___ na - ra - ga. When I'm with-out ___ you, I'm cra - zy. Ja eo -

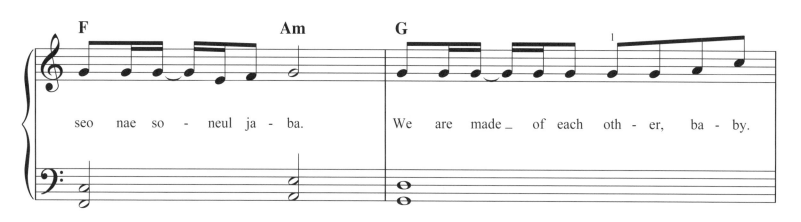

seo nae so - neul ja - ba. We are made ___ of each oth - er, ba - by.

You, you are my u - ni - verse ___ and ___ I just want to

put you first. ___ And you, you are my u - ni - verse ___ and you

make my world light up in - side. ____ My u - ni - verse. ____

My u - ni - verse. ____ My u - ni - verse.

You, you are my u - ni - verse ____ and ____ I... ____

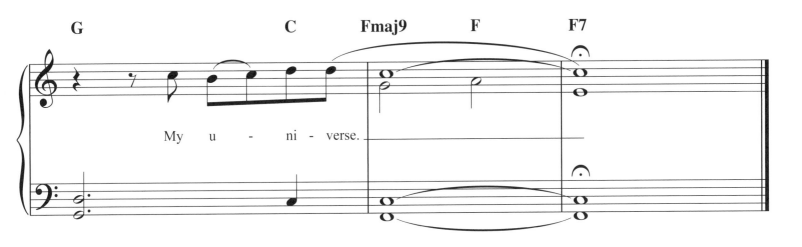

My u - ni - verse.

PERMISSION TO DANCE

Words and Music by ED SHEERAN,
JOHNNY McDAID, STEVE MAC
and JENNA ANDREWS

Bright Dance beat

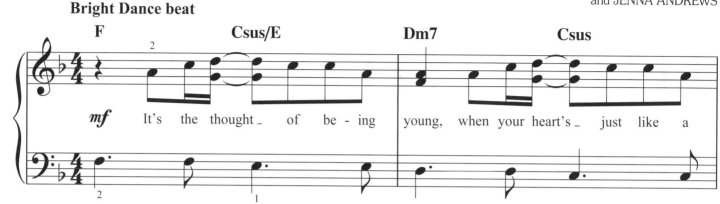

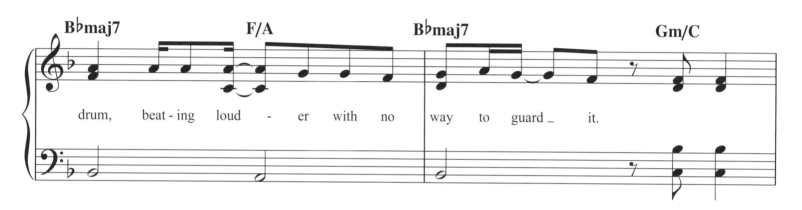

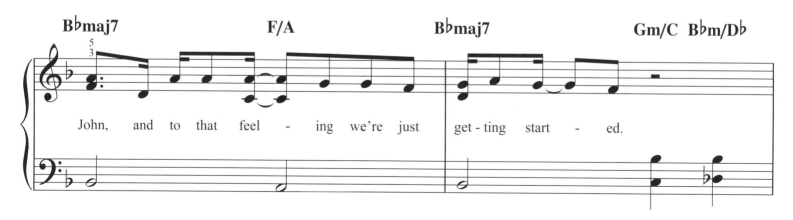

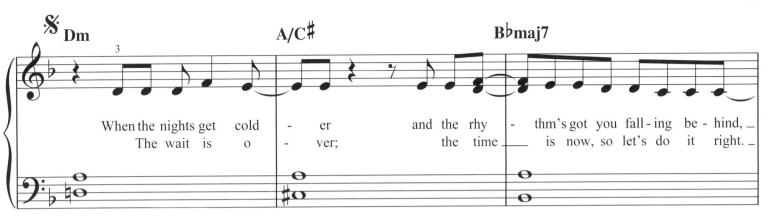

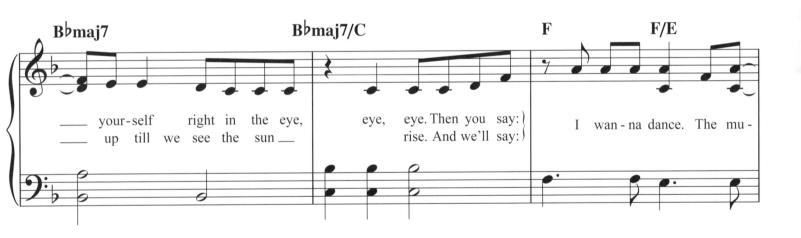

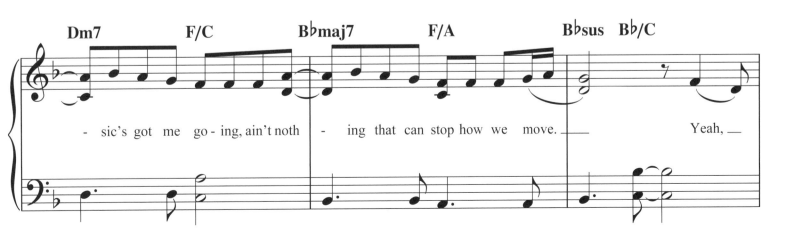

let's break our plans and live ___ just like we're gold-en and roll ___ in like we're danc-ing fools. ___

___ We don't need to wor - y, ___ 'cause when ___

___ we fall, we know how to land. ___ Don't need to talk the talk, just

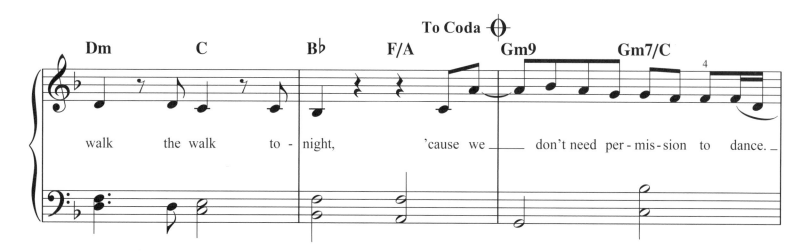

walk the walk to-night, 'cause we ___ don't need per-mis-sion to dance. ___

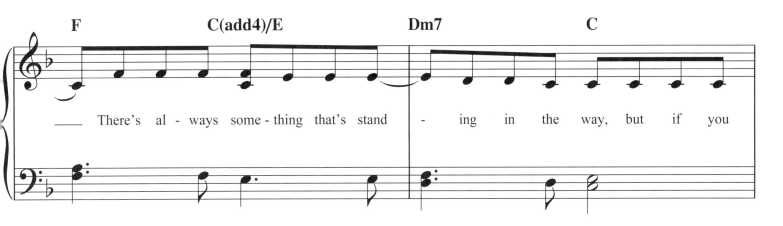

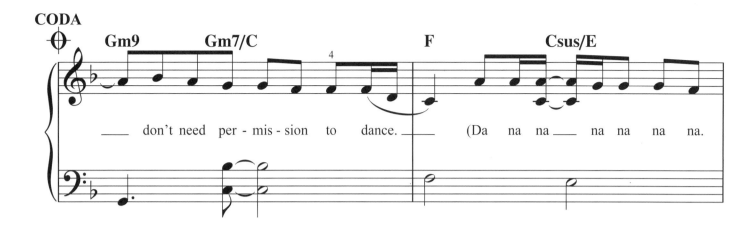

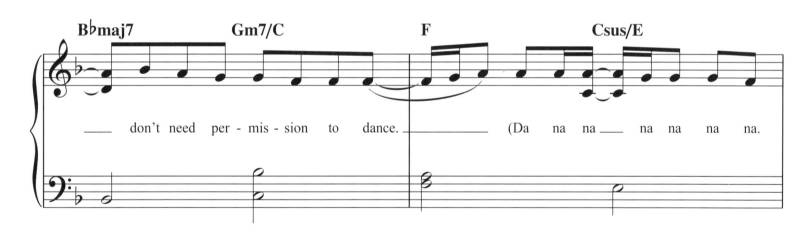

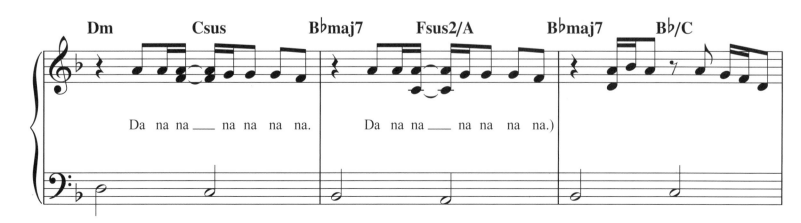

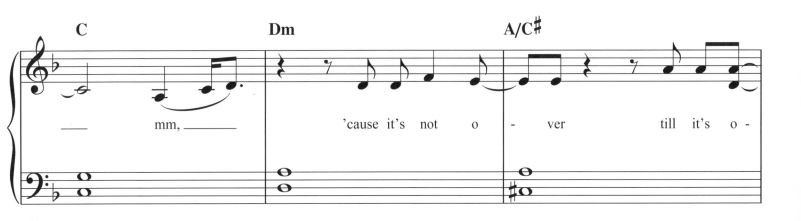

let's break our plans and live ____ just like we're gold-en and roll ____ in like we're danc - ing fools. ____

B♭/C **Dm7** **A7/C♯**

____ We don't need to wor - ry, ____ 'cause when ____

B♭maj7 **C** **F** **C/E**

____ we fall, we know how to land. ____ Don't need to talk the talk, just

Dm **C** **B♭** **Am** **Gm9** **Gm7/C**

walk the walk to - night, 'cause we ____ don't need per - mis - sion to dance.

STAY

Words and Music by JUSTIN BIEBER, BLAKE SLATKIN,
OMER FEDI, CHARLIE PUTH, CHARLTON HOWARD,
MAGNUS HOLBERG, MICHAEL MULE,
ISSAC DeBONI and SUBHAAN RAHMAN

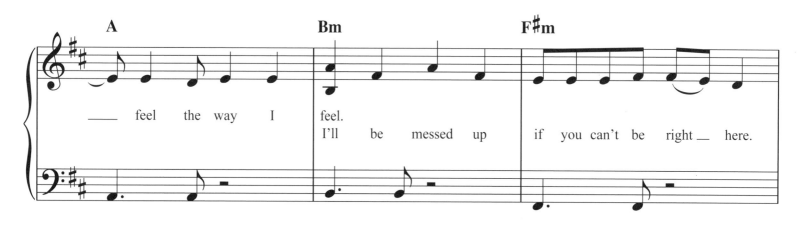

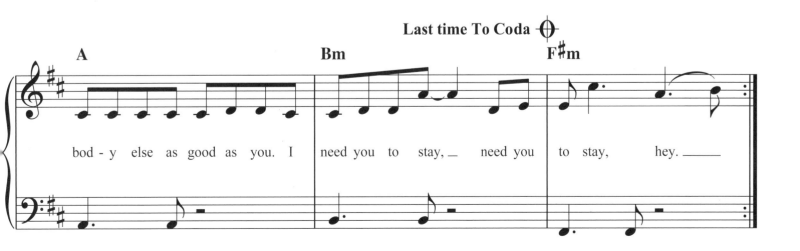

When I'm a - way from you, I miss your touch.

You're the rea - son I be -

lieve in love. _____

It's been dif - fi - cult for me to trust,

and I'm a - fraid that I'm - a mess it up. _____

Ain't no way _ that I can

leave you strand - ed,

'cause you ain't ev - er left me emp - ty - hand - ed.

And you know＿ that I know＿ that I can't＿ live with-out＿ you, so ba-by,

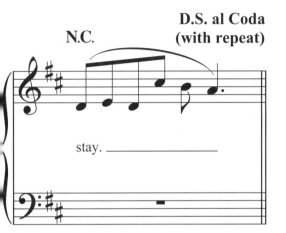

N.C.

stay.＿＿＿＿

D.S. al Coda (with repeat)

CODA

to stay, hey.＿

I need you to stay,＿ need you to stay, hey.＿＿

SHIVERS

Words and Music by ED SHEERAN,
JOHNNY McDAID, STEVE MAC
and KAL LAVELLE

Fast driving beat

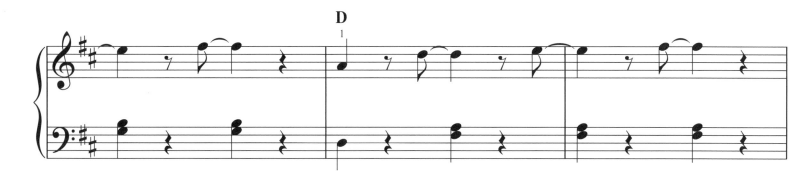

I took an ar - row to the heart.
car,

I nev - er kissed a mouth that taste like yours.
on the back __ seat in the moon - lit dark.

Straw - ber - ries __ and
Wrap me up __ be - tween your

some - thing more,
legs and arms,

ooh, yeah, I want it all.
ooh, I can't get e - nough.

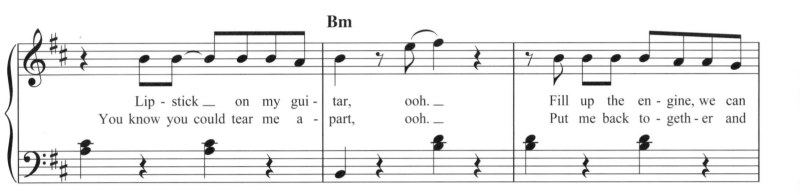

Lip - stick __ on my gui - tar,
You know you could tear me a - part,

ooh. __
ooh. __

Fill up the en - gine, we can
Put me back to - geth - er and

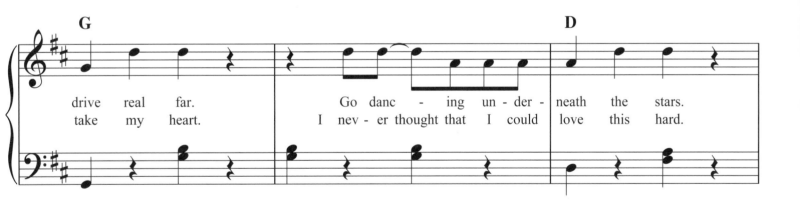

drive real far.
take my heart.

Go danc - ing un - der - neath the stars.
I nev - er thought that I could love this hard.

Ooh, yeah, I want it all. __
Ooh, I can't get e - nough.

Mmm, __ you got me feel - ing like
Ooh, __

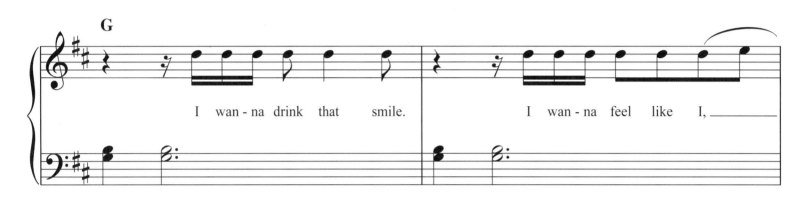

ooh, I love it when you do it like ____ that. And when you're

close up, ____ give me the shiv-ers. Oh, ba-by, you wan-na dance 'til the

sun-light cracks ____ and when they say the par-ty's o-ver then we'll

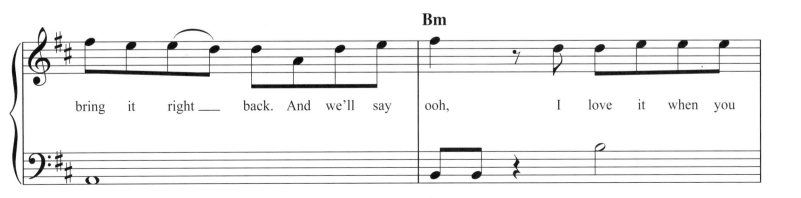

bring it right ____ back. And we'll say ooh, I love it when you

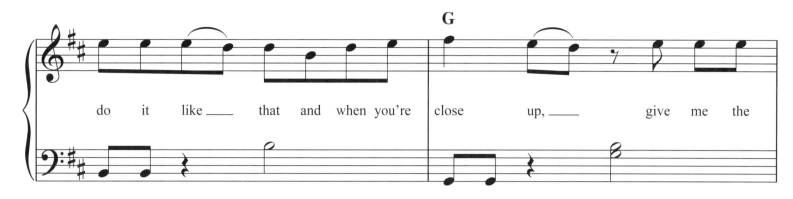

do it like ___ that and when you're close up, ___ give me the

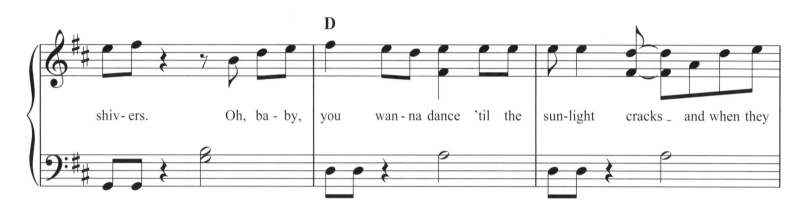

shiv-ers. Oh, ba-by, you wan-na dance 'til the sun-light cracks _ and when they

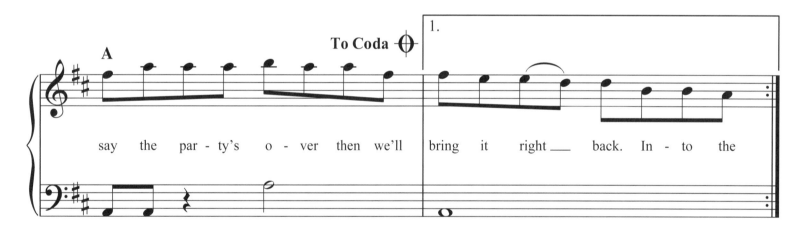

say the par-ty's o-ver then we'll bring it right ___ back. In-to the

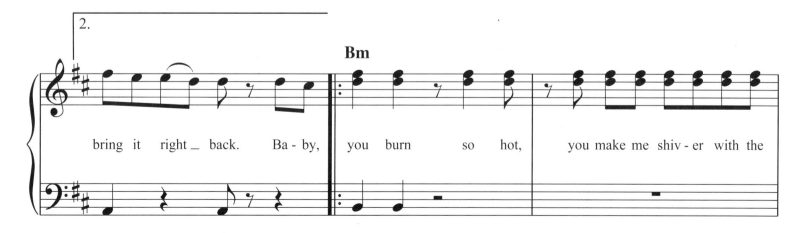

bring it right _ back. Ba-by, you burn so hot, you make me shiv-er with the

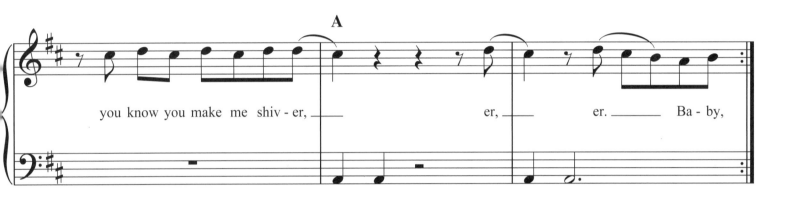

WE DON'T TALK ABOUT BRUNO

from ENCANTO

Music and Lyrics by
LIN-MANUEL MIRANDA

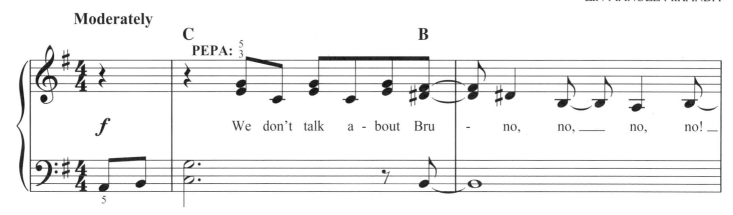

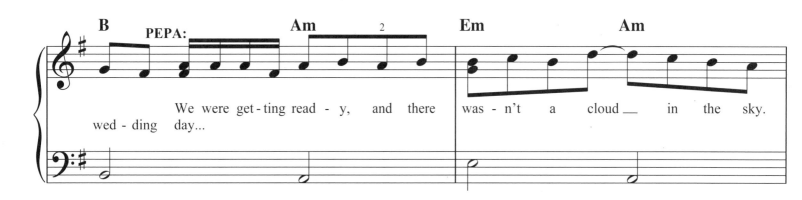

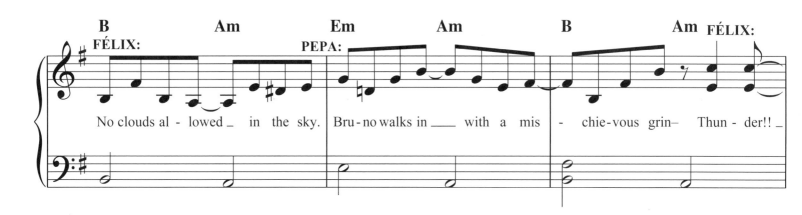

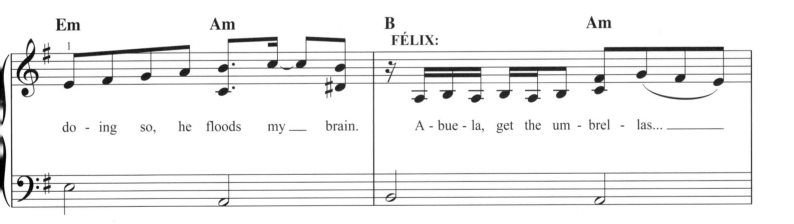

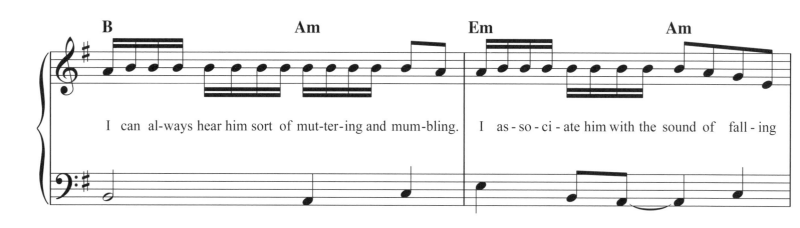

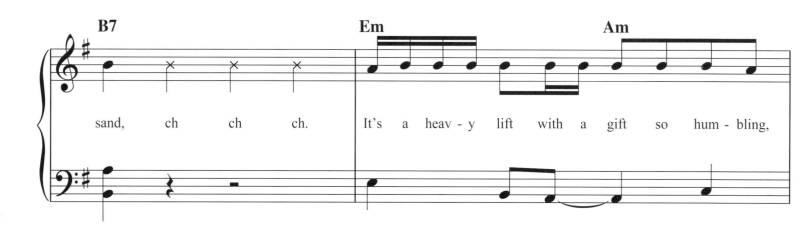

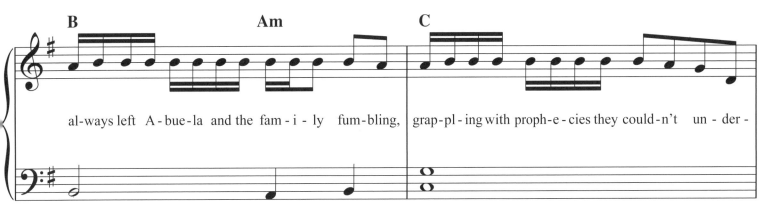

al-ways left A-bue-la and the fam-i-ly fum-bling, grap-pl-ing with proph-e-cies they could-n't un-der-

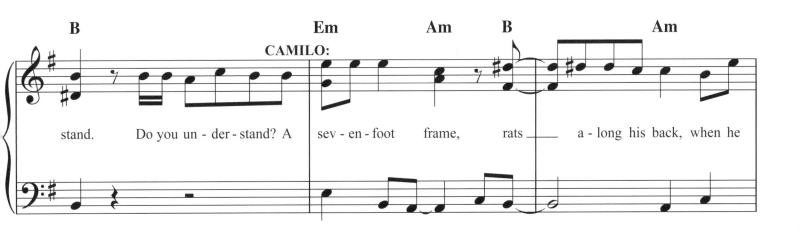

CAMILO:

stand. Do you un-der-stand? A sev-en-foot frame, rats ___ a-long his back, when he

calls your __ name it all __ fades _ to black. Yeah, he sees your __ dreams and feasts _

PEPA, FÉLIX,
CAMILO & DOLORES:

__ on __ your screams. We don't talk a-bout Bru - no, no, __ no, no!

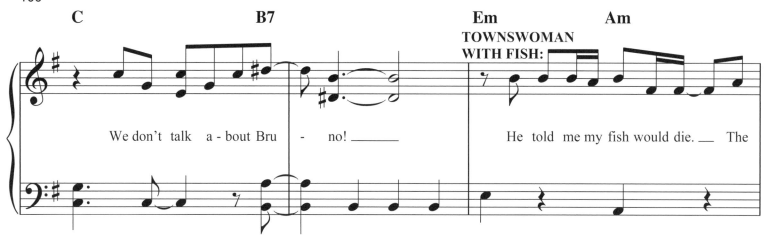

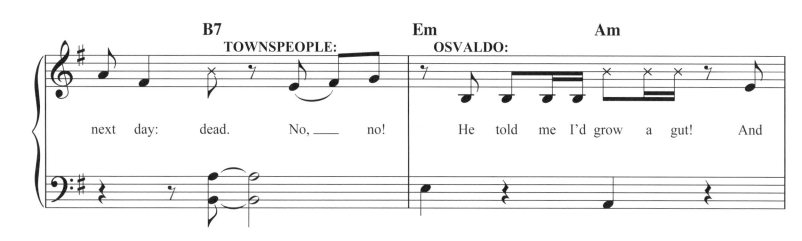

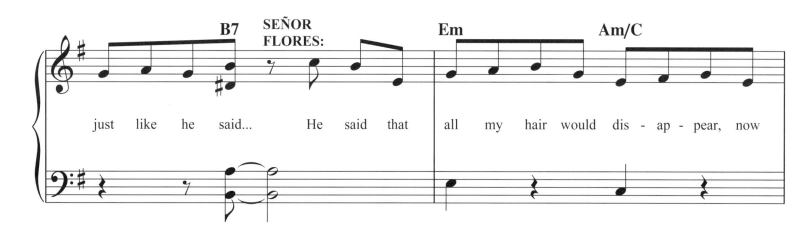

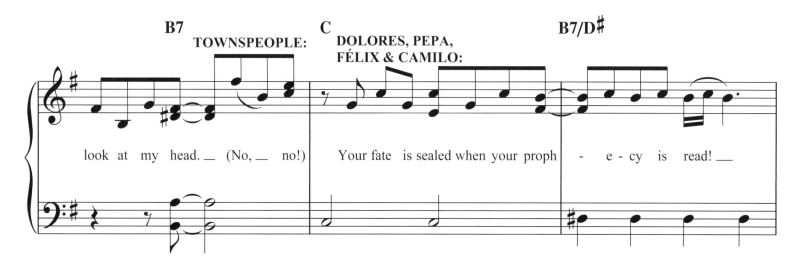

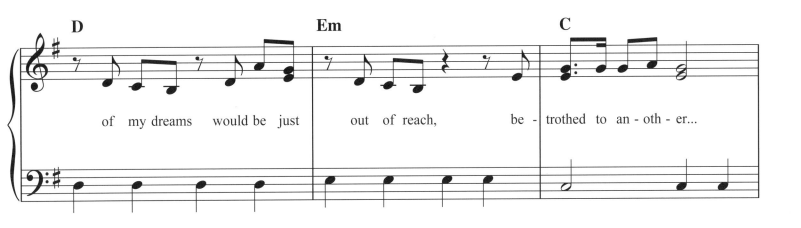

G   **2**   ISABELA: **D**   **3**   **Em**   **3**

It's like I hear him ___ now. Hey sis,   I want not a sound ___ out of you... ___

C   DOLORES: MIRABEL: **B**   **C**   **B**

___ I can hear him now! Um, Bru-no... Yeah, a-bout that Bru-no... I

C   **B**   **C**   **B**   CAMILO:

real-ly need to know a-bout Bru-no... Gim-me the truth and the whole truth, Bru-no! Is - a-

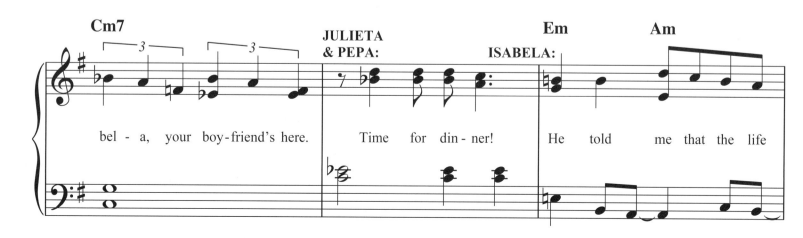

Cm7   JULIETA & PEPA: **Em**   **Am**   ISABELA:

bel - a, your boy-friend's here. Time for din - ner! He told me that the life

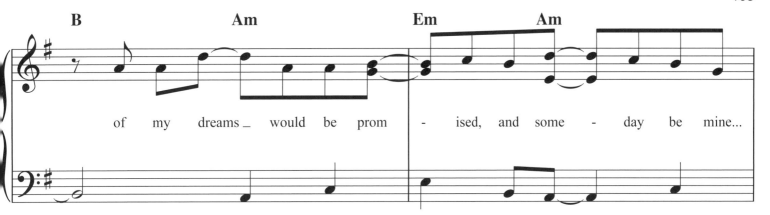

of my dreams _ would be prom - ised, and some - day be mine...

FÉLIX: No clouds al - lowed... _ **CAMILO:** Yeah, he sees your dreams and feasts _ on _ your screams.

PEPA: You tell - ing this sto - ry or _ am I? **ABUELA ALMA:** *Ó - ye,* Ma - ria - no's on his

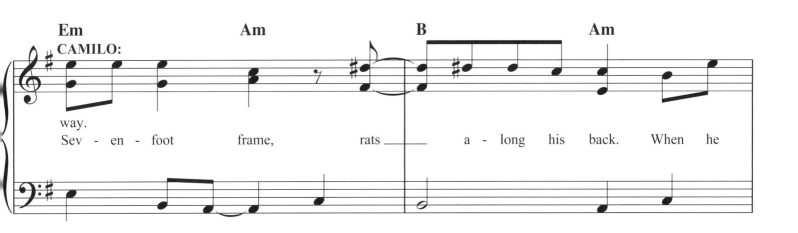

CAMILO: way. Sev - en - foot frame, rats _ a - long his back. When he

Em | Am | B | Am | Em | Am

calls your _ name it all _ fades _ to black. Yeah, he sees your _ dreams, and feasts _

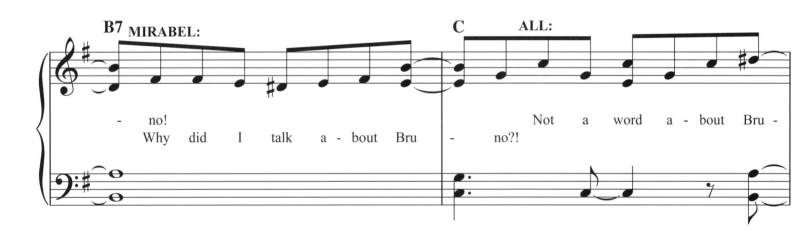

B | Am | C

AGUSTÍN, JULIETA & ABUELA ALMA: **ALL:**

_ on your screams. He's here! Don't talk a - bout Bru -

B7 **MIRABEL:** | C **ALL:**

- no! Not a word a - bout Bru -
Why did I talk a - bout Bru - no?!

B7 **MIRABEL:** | Em

- no!
Nev - er should - a brought up Bru - no!